WHISPERS FROM BEYOND

Healing Signs from Loved Ones and the Universe

By
Wendy Samons

Table of Contents

ABOUT THE AUTHOR

I am an independent publisher, lifelong learner, and deeply spiritual seeker who has dedicated my life to understanding the greater meaning of life. With a background in nursing and a personal journey profoundly shaped by the loss of my oldest son, Benjamin, I have found comfort and wisdom in the ways the universe communicates through signs, synchronicities, and moments of divine connection.

My writing emerges from the intersection of professional healthcare experience and profound personal loss, blending scientific understanding with spiritual insight. As a registered nurse, I witnessed countless moments where conventional medicine met unexplainable healing, where families found comfort in signs from departed loved ones, and where the mystery of consciousness revealed itself in ways that transcended clinical understanding.

The loss of Benjamin transformed my life in ways I never anticipated, opening my awareness to the subtle languages through which love communicates across the veil between worlds. What began as a personal quest for connection with my son evolved into a deeper exploration of how the universe speaks to all of us through meaningful coincidences, natural messengers, and the gentle whispers of divine guidance.

My approach combines compassionate wisdom with practical insight, helping readers develop their own capacity for recognizing and interpreting universal signs while maintaining a grounded perspective and professional support when needed. My work has been shaped by extensive research into neuroscience, particularly the groundbreaking work of Dr. Tara Swart on consciousness and pattern recognition, demonstrating how spiritual awareness and scientific understanding can complement and enhance each other.

When not writing, I enjoy flower gardening, exploring nature with my husband Gary, and cherishing time with our three Border Collie companions—Bella, Ayla, and Chloe. I find joy in travel and new adventures, practice yoga and water activities, and continue to seek wisdom in the extraordinary messages hidden within everyday life.

Through this book, I offer readers both the comfort of knowing they are not alone in their experiences with spiritual signs and practical tools for developing deeper awareness of the universe's constant communication. My message is simple yet profound: love never dies, and those we've lost continue to guide and comfort us through the language of signs, if only we learn to listen with both our hearts and minds

For my beloved son: *Benjamin Joseph Dominguez 1996-2015*

You were my world, my firstborn, my beautiful boy
You and I were one in the same.
The twinkle in your eyes when you smiled,
Your way with words.

How did I not know how much pain you were in?
You were so much fun, so smart, so giving and caring,
You had such a joyous heart.
Always helping others when you could.

How did I miss this?

Then there it was, that fateful, gloomy November day.
"Unconscious and unresponsive patient", said the dispatcher to
EMS.
It was way too soon Ben,
You weren't ready!

Maybe it wasn't your choice,
Or, maybe it was?
On the Other Side, were you asked or were you told?
That you would not be coming back without saying goodbye.
Or were you wanting to stay, as the intrigue of it all was too
difficult to escape?

Something shiny, something NEW Ben.
I am sure you would have run away so far, so fast from your
    ultimate demise,
Had you known what would happen that day.

You didn't want to hurt yourself or your family.
You didn't know how you would make me understand that "Your
son is a drug addict!"
I scowled at you for uttering those words.
Not understanding that it was no longer a choice but a physical

necessity.

You thought you could control that monkey on your back, that I
know.

How could I have been so naive?

Oh, what is it like Ben?

Your energy is everywhere, I feel it often.

You are the Cardinal pecking at the windows all times of the day,

You are the static in the faulty wires of the stereo system on
    Christmas.

Letting your joyous presence be known.

You are the chills I get when I imagine you and Leah in another
    lifetime together.

Like Romeo and Juliet,

Leah to your Benjamin.

That love together that you were robbed of,

That she too was robbed of.

You are the wind and the rainbows,

The hope left in this world.

Are you here, there and everywhere Ben?

Never a dull moment, just the way you like it,

How beautiful it must be.

Will you return in my lifetime?

Or will you greet me in heaven?

I know that you are proud of me for picking up the pieces,

For Peter especially.

"You were such a good Mom" you would say.

"It wasn't your fault! You didn't know!"

I lied to you Mom, over and over.

Just so that I wouldn't look bad in your eyes.

I wanted so much to change, but it got the best of me.

I just thought I could beat it.

But, yes, it is so beautiful Mom,
And I want to stay a while.
You have nothing to fear,

Be strong Mom!
I'd say, "I love you Ben". You would say, "I love you more".
I'd say, "I love you most". And you would say, "That is not
    possible".

I will be strong!
Until we meet again my dear son.

INTRODUCTION: WHEN SCIENCE MEETS SPIRIT

"The privilege of a lifetime is to become who you truly are." — Carl Jung

The morning after my son Benjamin passed away, I found myself standing in my garden, devastated and searching for any sign that his spirit lived on. As tears blurred my vision, a brilliant red cardinal landed on the fence directly in front of me and remained there for several minutes, its vibrant presence impossible to ignore. In my grief-stricken state, I dismissed this as mere coincidence. Yet over the following weeks, cardinals began appearing at the most poignant moments—when I was sorting through Benjamin's belongings, during my deepest moments of despair, and when I questioned whether I could find meaning in life again.

As a registered nurse, I had spent decades grounded in scientific evidence and medical protocol. The idea that my deceased son might be communicating through birds felt foreign to everything I had been trained to believe. Yet the emotional healing I experienced through these encounters couldn't be dismissed. These moments of connection became anchors of comfort in an ocean of grief, gradually transforming my understanding of life, death, and the mysterious ways love transcends physical boundaries.

It wasn't until I discovered the work of neuroscientist Dr. Tara Swart that I began to understand how both perspectives could coexist. In her groundbreaking research on consciousness and signs, Dr. Swart explains that our brains are naturally wired to seek meaning and recognize patterns through what she calls the Reticular Activating System (RAS)—a network in our brainstem that filters information and determines what reaches our conscious awareness. When we set intentions or focus on particular goals, our RAS begins prioritizing information that aligns with those intentions.

This scientific framework didn't diminish the spiritual significance of my experiences with cardinals; instead, it enriched my understanding of how the human brain and spirit work together to create meaning during times of profound loss and healing. Dr. Swart's research demonstrates that what may appear as "random signs" can actually represent our brain's sophisticated ability to draw attention to cues that help us navigate toward what we've asked the universe for.

The Intersection of Grief and Awareness

Modern neuroscience reveals that grief fundamentally alters our brain chemistry and perception. During periods of loss and trauma, our neural pathways become hypervigilant to potential sources of comfort and meaning. This heightened sensitivity, rather than being a sign of weakness or wishful thinking, may actually be an adaptive mechanism that opens us to forms of healing and connection we might otherwise miss.

Dr. Swart's research on neuroplasticity—the brain's ability to reorganize and form new neural connections—shows that consistent spiritual practices literally reshape our neural architecture. Each time we acknowledge a meaningful sign, express gratitude for a moment of connection, or act on intuitive guidance, we strengthen neural pathways that support both emotional resilience and spiritual awareness.

This understanding transforms how we approach messages from beyond. Rather than viewing them as either purely scientific phenomena or entirely spiritual experiences, we can embrace a more integrated perspective that honors both the neurological and transcendent aspects of these encounters.

A Personal Journey of Discovery

My background in healthcare initially made me skeptical of anything that couldn't be measured or quantified. Yet as I began documenting my experiences with cardinals, butterflies, and other meaningful signs, patterns emerged that challenged my purely rational worldview. The timing of these encounters, their emotional resonance, and their consistent appearance during moments of greatest need created a compelling case for something beyond mere coincidence.

The healing power of these experiences became undeniable. Each cardinal sighting brought a moment of peace. Every butterfly that appeared during difficult decisions seemed to offer gentle guidance. The white feathers I found in unlikely places provided reassurance during my darkest hours. While I couldn't prove these were messages from Benjamin, their therapeutic impact on my grieving heart was measurable and real.

Through my journey from skeptical healthcare professional to someone who embraces both scientific understanding and spiritual awareness, I've learned that healing often occurs at the intersection of evidence and faith, reason and intuition, the seen and unseen worlds.

The Language of Love Beyond Death

In the pages that follow, we'll explore how messages from loved ones who have crossed over serve as bridges between grief and healing, between despair and hope, between isolation and connection. These communications don't come with medical guarantees or scientific certifications, but they offer something equally valuable: the reminder that love is indeed stronger than death, and that those we've lost find ways to continue walking alongside us on our healing journey.

Dr. Swart's research provides crucial insight into why these experiences feel so authentic and transformative. When we understand how our brains process meaningful patterns and synchronicities, we can better discern between genuine spiritual guidance and our mind's natural tendency to seek comfort in random events. This discernment doesn't diminish the mystery of spiritual communication; rather, it helps us receive these messages with greater clarity and confidence.

Your Invitation to Healing

Whether you're navigating the loss of a loved one, seeking guidance during life's transitions, or simply curious about the ways the universe communicates with us, this book offers both practical tools and spiritual insights for recognizing and interpreting divine messages. You don't need special psychic abilities or religious training to receive these communications—you simply need an open heart and the willingness to notice the signs that surround you.

Each chapter provides a different lens for understanding how messages from beyond manifest in our lives. We'll explore the science behind synchronicity while honoring the sacred nature of spiritual connection. We'll learn to distinguish between authentic signs and wishful thinking while remaining open to possibilities beyond our current understanding.

Most importantly, we'll discover that healing doesn't require us to choose between scientific reasoning and spiritual awareness. Instead, true healing often occurs when we integrate both perspectives, allowing them to enhance and inform each other as we navigate our journey through loss toward wholeness.

A Note of Discernment

While this book explores the healing potential of spiritual messages, it's essential to understand that these experiences complement rather than replace professional mental health care or medical treatment. The signs and synchronicities we'll discuss can provide comfort, guidance, and emotional support during difficult times, but they should never substitute for appropriate professional care when dealing with serious grief, trauma, or health concerns.

The healing we explore in these pages refers primarily to emotional and spiritual recovery—the mending of broken hearts, the restoration of hope, and the renewal of connection with life's deeper meaning. Physical healing, when it occurs in conjunction with spiritual experiences, should always be understood within the context of comprehensive healthcare that includes qualified medical professionals.

As we embark on this journey together, may you find both comfort in the love that transcends death and confidence in your ability to recognize the gentle ways the universe reaches out to guide and heal us all.

The cardinal still visits my garden regularly, and each time I see its brilliant red flash among the green leaves, I'm reminded that love never dies—it simply learns new ways to make itself known

CHAPTER 1: THE NEUROSCIENCE OF SIGNS - WHEN BRAIN MEETS SOUL

"Your brain is your filter on reality. What you choose to notice creates your world." — Dr. Tara Swart

"Synchronicity is an ever-present reality for those who have eyes to see." — Carl Jung

Blake had always been a numbers person. As a software engineer, his world revolved around algorithms, data patterns, and logical sequences. So when the number 1111 began appearing repeatedly in his life during a period of career uncertainty, his analytical mind initially dismissed it as confirmation bias—the tendency to notice information that confirms our existing beliefs.

But the appearances became impossible to ignore. The sequence manifested on digital clocks during crucial decision-making moments, appeared on receipts when he was contemplating major life changes, and even showed up in lines of code when he was debugging programs. What made these occurrences particularly compelling wasn't just their frequency, but their uncanny timing—often coinciding with moments of deep contemplation about whether to leave his stable but unfulfilling corporate position to start his own technology consulting firm.

The turning point came during a particularly challenging week when Blake discovered that his employee ID number contained 1111, his new apartment address included those digits, and a potential client's phone number ended with the same sequence. When a friend texted him at exactly 11:11 PM with encouragement about his entrepreneurial dreams, Blake's scientific skepticism began to yield to the possibility that something beyond random chance was at work.

Dr. Tara Swart's research on the Reticular Activating System would explain Blake's experience through the lens of neuroscience. His RAS, primed by his career uncertainty and desire for guidance, began filtering his environment to highlight the numerical pattern that held significance for his current life situation. Yet the consistency and timing of these appearances suggested a dimension beyond simple pattern recognition—a collaboration between Blake's brain and what many would call divine guidance.

The Reticular Activating System: Our Internal Guidance Filter

At the base of our brainstem lies a remarkable neural network called the Reticular Activating System, which Dr. Swart describes as our brain's most sophisticated filtering mechanism. This network, roughly the size of a pencil, determines which of the millions of sensory inputs we encounter each day reach our conscious awareness and which remain in the background of our experience.

The RAS operates like a highly selective security guard for our consciousness, allowing only personally relevant information to pass through to our attention. When we're shopping for a particular car model, we suddenly notice that vehicle everywhere. When we're pregnant, we become aware of babies and pregnant women in ways we never noticed before. This isn't because these things have increased in frequency—it's because our RAS has been programmed to recognize them as significant.

Dr. Swart's groundbreaking insight is that spiritual experiences often operate through this same mechanism. When we're grieving, seeking guidance, or going through major life transitions, our RAS becomes highly attuned to potential sources of comfort, meaning, and direction. The cardinal that appears during a moment of longing for a deceased parent, the butterfly that crosses our path during a difficult decision, or the sequence of numbers that seems to follow us through challenging times—these experiences may represent our brain's remarkable ability to detect meaningful patterns in our environment.

This scientific understanding doesn't diminish the spiritual significance of these encounters. Rather, it reveals how our neurological and spiritual systems work in harmony, with the brain serving as a sophisticated instrument for recognizing divine communication when it occurs.

Neuroplasticity and Spiritual Awareness

One of Dr. Swart's most profound contributions to understanding spiritual experience is her research on neuroplasticity—the brain's ability to reorganize itself throughout our lives by forming new neural connections. This research reveals that spiritual practices don't just feel good; they literally reshape our brain structure in ways that enhance our capacity for awareness, compassion, and meaning-making.

When we consistently practice activities like meditation, gratitude, or mindful attention to signs and synchronicities, we strengthen neural pathways associated with these experiences. Each time we notice a meaningful coincidence and respond with appreciation, we reinforce brain circuits that make us more likely to recognize similar patterns in the future. This creates what neuroscientists call "positive neuroplasticity"—the brain's tendency to develop increasingly sophisticated abilities in areas we consistently practice.

The implications for spiritual development are profound. Rather than requiring innate psychic abilities, our capacity to recognize and interpret spiritual signs can be developed through consistent practice and attention. As Dr. Swart notes, "Each time we follow an inspired nudge, we strengthen new neural circuits, making it easier to trust our intuition the next time."

This neuroplasticity also explains why some people seem naturally more sensitive to spiritual signs while others struggle to notice them. Those who have cultivated practices of mindfulness, meditation, or spiritual awareness have literally trained their brains to be more receptive to subtle patterns and meaningful coincidences. Yet this capacity remains available to everyone, regardless of their starting point or previous experience.

The Science of Meaningful Coincidences

Carl Jung's concept of synchronicity—meaningful coincidences that feel too significant to be random—finds new understanding through contemporary neuroscience. While Jung described synchronicity as an "acausal connecting principle" that operates beyond normal cause-and-effect relationships, Dr. Swart's research suggests that our brains play a crucial role in both recognizing and creating these meaningful connections.

The phenomenon begins with what neuroscientists call "pattern recognition"—our brain's ability to detect relationships and similarities across different experiences. This capacity, which evolved to help our ancestors survive by recognizing dangers and opportunities in their environment, now operates in more subtle ways to help us navigate complex emotional and spiritual terrain.

When we're facing difficult decisions or processing grief, our pattern recognition systems become hypervigilant to potential sources of guidance or comfort. The brain begins scanning our environment more intensively for relevant information, making us more likely to notice coincidences that align with our current needs or concerns.

However, the neurological explanation doesn't account for the full mystery of synchronicity. The precise timing, emotional resonance, and often impossible odds of meaningful coincidences suggest that something beyond random pattern recognition may be at work. As Dr. Swart acknowledges, understanding the brain's role in spiritual experience reveals "how body, mind, and spirit work together to guide us," rather than explaining away the mystery of spiritual connection.

The Grief Brain: Heightened Sensitivity to Signs

Recent neuroscientific research has revealed that grief creates specific changes in brain structure and function that may enhance our ability to perceive spiritual signs. The intense emotional state of loss triggers heightened activity in regions associated with memory, attachment, and meaning-making, creating what researchers describe as a "hypervigilant" state of awareness.

This heightened sensitivity serves an important evolutionary function—it helps us detect potential threats and sources of support during vulnerable periods. But it also opens us to subtle environmental cues that might otherwise escape our notice. The grieving brain, seeking connection and comfort, becomes exceptionally attuned to experiences that might represent continued contact with lost loved ones.

Dr. Swart's research suggests that this neurological state doesn't represent wishful thinking or psychological disturbance, but rather an adaptive response that can facilitate healing when properly understood. The key lies in developing discernment—learning to distinguish between meaningful signs and random coincidences while remaining open to genuine spiritual communication.

Many people report that their first profound spiritual experiences occur during periods of intense grief or loss. The cardinal that appears at a funeral, the butterfly that visits during the anniversary of a loved one's death, or the song that plays at precisely the moment we're thinking of someone we've lost—these experiences often mark the beginning of a deeper spiritual awareness that continues long after the acute phase of grief has passed.

Case Study: Sarah's Healing Journey

Sarah's story illustrates how understanding the neuroscience of signs can enhance rather than diminish their healing power. Six months after losing her husband to cancer, Sarah began experiencing what she initially dismissed as "wishful thinking"—a series of meaningful coincidences that seemed to offer comfort and guidance during her darkest moments.

The experiences began with music. Songs that held special meaning for her and her husband began playing at emotionally significant moments—when she was struggling with loneliness, contemplating major decisions, or feeling overwhelmed by the practical demands of widowhood. At first, Sarah attributed these occurrences to radio programming coincidence, but the specificity and timing of these musical messages gradually convinced her that something more meaningful was occurring.

When Sarah learned about Dr. Swart's research on the RAS, she began keeping a journal of these musical encounters, noting her emotional state, the circumstances of each occurrence, and any decisions or insights that followed. The patterns that emerged revealed a sophisticated system of guidance that seemed to address her specific needs with remarkable precision.

Rather than diminishing the spiritual significance of these experiences, understanding their neurological basis helped Sarah receive them with greater confidence and clarity. She realized that her brain's heightened sensitivity to meaningful music represented a collaboration between her neurological grief response and her husband's continued presence in her life. This integrated understanding accelerated her healing process and helped her make better decisions during a challenging life transition.

Developing Discernment: Science-Based Guidelines

Dr. Swart's research provides valuable guidelines for distinguishing between meaningful spiritual signs and random coincidences that our pattern-seeking brains might misinterpret as significant:

- **Emotional Resonance:** Authentic spiritual signs typically produce immediate feelings of peace, recognition, or clarity, rather than anxiety or confusion. The body's response often provides more reliable information than mental analysis.
- **Timing Correlation:** Meaningful signs usually correlate with relevant life circumstances, emotional states, or specific questions

we've been contemplating. Random coincidences lack this contextual relevance.

- **Behavioral Impact:** Genuine spiritual guidance typically inspires positive action or provides clarity about previously confusing situations. Signs that create paralysis or increase anxiety may represent fear-based thinking rather than authentic guidance.
- **Consistency Without Obsession:** Meaningful patterns appear consistently but don't create compulsive behavior or interfere with daily functioning. Healthy spiritual awareness enhances life rather than dominating it.
- **Integration with Practical Wisdom:** Authentic spiritual signs complement rather than contradict sound judgment, professional advice, and practical considerations. Divine guidance typically supports our highest good, which includes attending to real-world responsibilities and relationships.

The Collaborative Model: Brain and Spirit Working Together

Dr. Swart's most significant contribution to understanding spiritual experience may be her "collaborative model"—the idea that spiritual awareness represents a partnership between our neurological capacities and transcendent intelligence. Rather than viewing science and spirituality as opposing explanations for meaningful coincidences, this model suggests they work together to create experiences that are both neurologically valid and spiritually authentic.

This collaboration manifests in several ways:

- **Enhanced Pattern Recognition:** Spiritual practices like meditation and prayer improve our brain's ability to detect subtle patterns and meaningful connections, making us better instruments for receiving divine guidance.
- **Improved Emotional Regulation:** Regular spiritual practice strengthens neural circuits associated with calm awareness and emotional balance, creating optimal conditions for receiving and interpreting spiritual signs.
- **Increased Cognitive Flexibility:** Spiritual awareness enhances our ability to consider multiple perspectives and possibilities, helping us interpret signs in ways that serve our highest good.

- **Strengthened Intuitive Capabilities:** Practices that quiet mental chatter and enhance present-moment awareness develop our capacity to access forms of knowing that operate beyond linear thinking.

Blake's story demonstrates how this integrated approach can transform both career decisions and spiritual understanding. By combining analytical thinking with openness to meaningful patterns, he successfully navigated a major life transition while developing a more nuanced understanding of how the universe communicates through our daily experience.

His software consulting firm thrived beyond his expectations, validating his interpretation of 1111 as encouragement to trust his entrepreneurial instincts. More importantly, the experience taught him that scientific understanding and spiritual awareness can enhance each other, creating a more complete framework for navigating life's complexities.

CHAPTER 2: SACRED SYMBOLS THROUGH TIME

"Symbols are the language of the soul." — Carl Jung

"What you seek is seeking you." — Rumi

Isla had always been drawn to spirals. As an architectural designer, she found herself incorporating spiral staircases, curved pathways, and circular windows into her projects with an almost unconscious compulsion. Her clients appreciated these organic elements, but Isla herself couldn't explain why these forms felt so essential to her creative process.

During a particularly challenging period in her career—when she questioned whether her architectural work held any deeper meaning—Isla took a morning walk through her neighborhood botanical garden. Her mind churned with self-doubt and career uncertainty as she wandered the winding paths. That's when she encountered a sunflower in full bloom, its center displaying a perfect spiral pattern that seemed to pulse with mathematical precision.

Fascinated, Isla knelt to examine the flower more closely. The spiral drew her attention inward, and for the first time in months, her anxious thoughts quieted. In that moment of stillness, she felt a profound sense of recognition— as if this pattern contained a message she desperately needed to receive.

Later that day, driven by curiosity, Isla researched the mathematics of spirals and discovered the Fibonacci sequence that governs much of nature's growth patterns. She learned that spirals represent evolution, expansion, and the journey of consciousness—concepts that resonated deeply with her current life questions. This discovery led her to explore other sacred symbols that appeared throughout architectural history, from ancient stone circles to Gothic cathedral rose windows.

Dr. Tara Swart's research on pattern recognition helps explain why certain symbols carry such powerful psychological impact. Our brains are naturally programmed to respond to specific geometric forms that appear consistently in nature and human culture. The spiral, in particular, activates neural pathways associated with growth, movement, and transformation—precisely the energies Isla needed during her period of professional transition.

Yet the timing of Isla's sunflower encounter, combined with its profound emotional impact, suggests that symbolic recognition operates on levels beyond simple pattern identification. Sacred symbols seem to appear in our awareness precisely when we need their particular wisdom, creating experiences of guidance that feel both psychologically meaningful and spiritually authentic.

The Universal Language of Sacred Geometry

Throughout human history, certain geometric forms have appeared consistently across cultures, suggesting that these symbols tap into fundamental structures of consciousness itself. Sacred geometry—the study of geometric patterns that reveal divine proportion and cosmic order—bridges the gap between mathematical precision and spiritual meaning.

Dr. Swart's research reveals that our brains respond to geometric patterns through neural networks associated with both aesthetic appreciation and meaning-making. When we encounter symbols like the golden spiral, the flower of life, or the vesica piscis, multiple brain regions activate simultaneously, creating experiences that are both beautiful and significant.

The golden ratio (approximately 1.618), found in spiral shells, flower petals, and human facial proportions, creates a sense of natural harmony that our brains recognize as inherently pleasing. This mathematical relationship appears so consistently in nature that many traditions consider it evidence of divine intelligence embedded in the physical world.

The Spiral: Symbol of Evolution and Return

The spiral represents perhaps the most universal sacred symbol, appearing in ancient petroglyphs, Celtic art, Islamic architecture, and contemporary spiritual practices. Unlike a circle, which returns to its starting point, the spiral suggests movement and growth while maintaining connection to its origin.

In psychological terms, the spiral represents the journey of individuation— our lifelong process of becoming who we truly are. Each cycle of the spiral represents a new level of understanding, where we revisit familiar themes with greater wisdom and perspective. This explains why spiral symbolism often appears during periods of personal growth or life transition.

The Mandala: Cosmic Order and Personal Integration

The mandala—a circular design radiating from a central point—appears in Hindu and Buddhist traditions, Navajo sand paintings, and Gothic cathedral rose windows. Carl Jung discovered that his patients spontaneously drew mandala-like images during healing processes, suggesting that these circular patterns represent psychological integration and wholeness.

Neuroscience reveals that creating or contemplating mandalas activates brain regions associated with focus, emotional regulation, and self-awareness. The symmetrical patterns create a meditative state that calms mental chatter and enhances access to deeper wisdom. This explains why mandala symbolism often appears as a sign during times of emotional healing or spiritual awakening.

Historical Context: Symbols as Bridges Between Worlds

Ancient cultures understood symbols as bridges between the physical and spiritual realms—visual forms that could convey truths too complex for words. These societies developed sophisticated symbolic languages that encoded wisdom about cosmology, psychology, and spiritual development in forms that could be transmitted across generations.

Egyptian Sacred Symbols

Ancient Egypt's symbolic system remains one of history's most comprehensive spiritual languages. The ankh represents the union of masculine and feminine principles, matter and spirit, death and eternal life. The Eye of Horus symbolizes protection, healing, and the ability to see beyond surface appearances. The scarab beetle represents transformation and renewal through its metamorphosis from larva to winged adult.

Dr. Swart's research suggests that these symbols remain psychologically active because they address universal human experiences—love, death, transformation, and the search for meaning—that activate the same neural networks today as they did thousands of years ago.

Celtic Sacred Geometry

Celtic culture created intricate knotwork patterns that represent the interconnectedness of all life. These endless knots, with no beginning or end, symbolize eternity and the continuous flow of energy through all existence. The triskelion (triple spiral) represents the three realms of existence—land, sea, and sky—as well as the three aspects of the divine feminine.

These symbols often appear as signs during times when we need reminding of our connection to larger patterns of meaning and belonging. Their appearance in dreams, meditation, or daily life may signal the importance of remembering our place in the web of existence.

Sacred Architecture as Symbolic Message

Gothic cathedrals, Hindu temples, and Islamic mosques embed sacred symbols in their very structure, creating architectural environments that communicate spiritual truths through form and proportion. The pointed arches of Gothic architecture direct attention upward toward transcendence, while the sacred geometry of their floor plans creates mandalas in stone.

When we encounter these architectural symbols—whether in person or through images—our brains respond to their embedded proportions and patterns, often triggering experiences of awe, reverence, or spiritual connection. These responses suggest that sacred architecture continues to function as intended, serving as a medium for spiritual communication across centuries.

Personal Symbol Recognition: Developing Your Sacred Alphabet

While universal symbols carry collective meanings, each individual also develops a personal symbolic vocabulary based on their unique experiences, cultural background, and spiritual journey. Learning to recognize your personal symbols enhances your ability to receive and interpret guidance from beyond.

Creating a Symbol Journal

Isla's architectural journey illustrates how personal symbol recognition develops through attention and practice. After her sunflower spiral experience, she began documenting symbols that appeared in her dreams, meditation, and daily life. She noticed that certain geometric forms—particularly spirals and circles—appeared consistently during periods of creative breakthrough or important decisions.

Over time, Isla's symbol journal revealed a sophisticated communication system between her conscious mind and deeper sources of wisdom. Triangles appeared when she needed to focus her energy and take decisive action. Squares showed up during times requiring stability and grounding. Circles emerged when she needed to embrace wholeness and completion.

Integration with Professional Life

Understanding her personal symbolic language transformed Isla's architectural practice. She began consciously incorporating symbols that held meaning for her clients based on their life circumstances and healing needs. A meditation center featured spiral pathways that supported contemplative journeying. A grief counseling center included circular gathering spaces that promoted emotional integration and support.

This integration of personal symbolism with professional work created architecture that served as healing environments, demonstrating how understanding sacred symbols can enhance our ability to serve others through our unique talents and skills.

Dr. Swart's Perspective: The Neuroscience of Symbolic Recognition

Dr. Swart's research reveals that symbolic recognition operates through the same neural networks involved in pattern recognition, emotional processing, and memory formation. When we encounter personally meaningful symbols, multiple brain regions activate simultaneously, creating rich, multidimensional experiences that combine visual perception with emotional resonance and intuitive insight.

This neurological understanding explains why certain symbols consistently trigger profound psychological responses across different individuals and cultures. The brain recognizes these patterns as significant not just intellectually, but through deep evolutionary programming that associates specific forms with survival, meaning, and transcendence.

The Reticular Activating System and Symbol Recognition

The RAS plays a crucial role in symbolic awareness by filtering our environment for personally relevant symbolic information. When we become consciously aware of our symbolic vocabulary—the forms that carry special meaning for us—our RAS begins highlighting these patterns in our daily experience.

This explains why people often report increased symbol sightings after beginning spiritual practices or going through significant life transitions. Their RAS, primed by intention and emotional significance, becomes more adept at detecting symbolic messages that might have previously escaped conscious awareness.

Neuroplasticity and Symbolic Development

Regular attention to symbolic messages literally rewires our brains to become more sensitive to this form of communication. Each time we notice a meaningful symbol and reflect on its relevance to our current life situation, we strengthen neural pathways associated with symbolic recognition and interpretation.

This neuroplasticity suggests that our capacity for receiving symbolic guidance can be developed through practice and attention. Those who consistently work with symbols—through meditation, dream work, or contemplative practices—develop increasingly sophisticated abilities to recognize and interpret symbolic communications.

Interpreting Ancient Symbols in Contemporary Life

Ancient symbols continue to resonate deeply in our modern world, speaking to us through art, technology, and spiritual practices with meanings as profound today as they were thousands of years ago. These enduring symbols serve as bridges between our contemporary experience and the timeless wisdom of our ancestors, offering guidance and insight for navigating modern life.

In today's digital age, we find ancient symbols seamlessly integrated into the technology that connects our world. The Bluetooth symbol, for instance, combines two Viking runes representing 'H' and 'B'—a deliberate choice by creator Jim Kardach to honor King Harold "Bluetooth" Gormsson, who united Danish tribes. This marriage of ancient symbolism with cutting-edge technology demonstrates how historical meanings can evolve while maintaining their essential connection to unity and communication.

The psychological impact of these ancient symbols remains powerful in contemporary life. Carl Jung's research into archetypes and the collective unconscious revealed how symbols tap into deep reservoirs of shared human experience. When we encounter symbols like the Egyptian Ankh or the Eye of Horus in modern contexts—whether in jewelry, tattoos, or spiritual practices—we're connecting with archetypal meanings that transcend time and culture.

In wellness and personal growth practices, ancient symbols continue to play vital roles. The Ankh, representing life and immortality in Egyptian tradition, appears frequently in modern healing sessions and meditation practices. The Phoenix, with its message of renewal and transformation, resonates particularly strongly in contemporary personal development contexts, offering hope and inspiration for those navigating life's challenges.

However, interpreting ancient symbols in contemporary life requires both knowledge and discernment. Understanding their historical context and original meanings provides a foundation for meaningful modern application. The Triskelion, for example, traditionally represented the three realms of earth, water, and sky, but today might speak to the integration of body, mind, and spirit in holistic wellness practices.

As we conclude this exploration of sacred symbols through time, we find ourselves standing at a remarkable intersection between ancient wisdom and modern understanding. The enduring power of these symbols—from the spirals of Celtic art to the geometric patterns of sacred architecture—demonstrates their continued relevance in our contemporary spiritual journey.

Isla's story reminds us that sacred symbols continue to speak to modern seekers, offering guidance and insight in surprisingly personal ways. Her experience with the spiral pattern reflects a universal truth: these sacred markers are not mere historical artifacts but living languages that continue to evolve and communicate divine wisdom.

The symbols we've explored form an unbroken chain of spiritual communication linking us to our ancestors while remaining vitally relevant today. They remind us that certain truths transcend time and culture, speaking to the deepest parts of human experience and consciousness.

Perhaps most importantly, we've learned that sacred symbols are not static or fixed in meaning, but rather living embodiments of spiritual truth that continue to reveal new layers of understanding to each generation. They invite us to engage with them personally, finding fresh relevance in their ancient forms while honoring their traditional significance.

As we move forward, may we remain open to the guidance these eternal symbols offer, recognizing them as waymarkers on our spiritual path. Their presence in our lives—whether through art, meditation, or spontaneous encounters—reminds us that we are part of an enduring tradition of seeking and finding divine wisdom through sacred signs and symbols.

CHAPTER 3: WINGED MESSENGERS - WHEN LOVE TAKES FLIGHT

"When cardinals appear, angels are near." — Traditional saying

"The butterfly counts not months but moments, and has time enough." — Rabindranath Tagore

Among all the ways our departed loved ones reach across the veil to comfort us, none are more universally recognized or emotionally powerful than the appearance of winged messengers. Cardinals with their brilliant red plumage, butterflies in their delicate dance of transformation, dragonflies shimmering with iridescent light, and feathers appearing in the most unlikely places—these gentle emissaries seem to carry love itself on their wings, arriving precisely when our hearts need them most.

Dr. Tara Swart's research on the Reticular Activating System helps explain why these particular messengers feel so significant. When we're grieving or seeking connection with loved ones who have passed, our RAS becomes attuned to symbols of hope, beauty, and transcendence. The sight of a cardinal's flash of red or a butterfly's graceful flight triggers neural pathways associated with comfort and meaning, creating what Swart describes as "meaningful pattern recognition" rather than mere coincidence.

Yet the consistency of these experiences across cultures and individuals suggests something beyond simple neuroscience. The timing, behavior, and emotional resonance of these encounters often transcend what we might expect from random wildlife encounters, carrying a quality of intentional communication that speaks directly to the heart.

Cardinals: Fiery Messengers of Eternal Love

The cardinal holds a special place in the realm of spiritual messengers, its vibrant red color symbolizing the eternal flame of love that death cannot extinguish. In Christian tradition, the cardinal represents the blood of Christ and the promise of eternal life. Native American cultures see the cardinal as a symbol of devotion, renewal, and the connection between earth and sky. But perhaps most meaningfully, countless grieving individuals have found comfort in the cardinal's consistent appearance during their darkest hours.

Maria's Story: A Father's Daily Visit

Three months after Maria's father passed away from cancer, she was struggling with the emptiness of his absence. Every morning for forty years, he had called to check on her and share the day's plans. Now, silence filled those precious morning moments, leaving her feeling abandoned and alone.

One particularly difficult morning, as Maria sat at her kitchen table weeping into her coffee, a brilliant red cardinal landed on the windowsill directly in front of her. The bird remained there for several minutes, tilting its head as if studying her face. When she reached toward the window, rather than flying away, the cardinal tapped gently on the glass with its beak before finally departing.

The next morning, the cardinal returned at exactly the same time. And the next. Soon, Maria realized that her father's morning visits hadn't ended—they had simply taken a different form. The cardinal's daily appearances became a source of profound comfort, maintaining their connection through the language of love that transcends physical boundaries.

From a neuroscientific perspective, Dr. Swart would explain that Maria's brain, primed by grief to seek connection and comfort, became highly attuned to the cardinal's presence. Her RAS, focused on maintaining her bond with her father, recognized the bird's consistent timing and behavior as meaningful rather than random. This recognition didn't diminish the spiritual significance of her experience—it illuminated how our brains and spirits work together to facilitate healing.

The Behavioral Evidence

What makes cardinal encounters particularly compelling is their frequent deviation from typical bird behavior. Cardinals that linger longer than natural, appear at emotionally significant moments, or display unusual fearlessness around humans often carry a quality that transcends ordinary wildlife encounters. These behavioral anomalies, combined with their emotional timing, create experiences that feel unmistakably intentional.

Cardinals also mate for life, a characteristic that resonates deeply with those mourning the loss of a life partner. Their year-round presence in many regions means they can serve as consistent messengers, providing ongoing comfort rather than seasonal visits. The male cardinal's protective behavior toward his mate and offspring mirrors the continued protective love many feel from departed spouses or parents.

Monarch Butterflies: Souls in Flight

The monarch butterfly carries perhaps the most powerful symbolism of any winged messenger, representing the soul's journey through transformation and rebirth. Ancient Greeks used the same word, *psyche*, to mean both "soul" and "butterfly," recognizing the profound connection between these delicate creatures and the human spirit's eternal nature.

The monarch's remarkable migration journey—spanning thousands of miles across multiple generations—serves as a metaphor for the soul's own journey beyond physical boundaries. Their transformation from caterpillar to chrysalis to butterfly mirrors the transition our loved ones make from physical form to spiritual essence, reminding us that death is not an ending but a beautiful metamorphosis.

Janet's Miracle Garden

Janet had always shared a passion for gardening with her mother, Rose, who passed away suddenly from a stroke. In their final conversation, Rose had expressed disappointment that her butterfly garden hadn't attracted many visitors that summer. Feeling this as unfinished business, Janet decided to expand her mother's garden as a living memorial.

On the first anniversary of Rose's death, Janet was working in the expanded butterfly garden, planting the last of the native flowers they had chosen together. As she patted soil around the final plant, she noticed a single monarch butterfly approaching. Rather than the typical brief visit, this butterfly began an elaborate dance around the garden, landing on each newly planted flower as if conducting an inspection.

Within minutes, more monarchs appeared—first three, then seven, then too many to count. For nearly an hour, Janet stood surrounded by dozens of monarch butterflies, all moving through the garden in what felt like a celebration of life and renewal. Neighbors later remarked they had never seen such a concentration of monarchs in their area, making the timing of this visitation even more remarkable.

Dr. Swart's research suggests that Janet's brain, focused on honoring her mother's memory through the garden project, became exceptionally receptive to butterfly appearances. Her RAS, primed by grief and love, recognized the monarchs' unusual behavior and timing as significant. Yet the sheer magnitude of the event—dozens of butterflies appearing simultaneously in unprecedented numbers—suggests a dimension beyond simple neural pattern recognition.

The Science of Synchronicity

The monarch's annual migration involves navigational abilities that still mystify scientists. These butterflies, weighing less than a paperclip, travel thousands of miles to destinations they have never seen, guided by magnetic fields, solar positions, and inherited cellular memory. This remarkable navigation ability makes their appearance at emotionally significant moments even more intriguing—are these encounters guided by the same mysterious forces that guide their epic journeys?

From a healing perspective, the monarch butterfly's message is particularly powerful for those struggling with the permanence of death. Their metamorphosis reminds us that transformation, while requiring the dissolution of familiar forms, leads to beauty, freedom, and new possibilities. The sight of a monarch's graceful flight can shift our perspective from loss to transformation, from ending to continuation.

Dragonflies: Guardians Between Worlds

Dragonflies, with their ability to hover, dart, and change direction instantly, symbolize adaptability, spiritual insight, and the capacity to see beyond surface illusions. Their iridescent wings catch and reflect light in rainbow patterns, earning them recognition as messengers of hope and transformation across many cultures.

In Japanese tradition, dragonflies represent courage, happiness, and the ability to move between realms. Native American cultures associate dragonflies with renewal, positive change, and the souls of loved ones. Their unique ability to fly in all directions makes them symbols of spiritual freedom and the unbounded nature of consciousness.

David's Transition Guide

David was facing one of the most difficult decisions of his life—whether to leave his corporate career to pursue his dream of becoming a teacher. The financial security of his current position provided for his family, but the work left him feeling empty and disconnected from his purpose. His deceased grandfather, a beloved educator, had always encouraged David to follow his passion for teaching.

For weeks, David struggled with the decision, seeking signs or guidance about the right path forward. One evening, while journaling about his dilemma in his backyard, a large dragonfly appeared and began circling his patio. Unlike typical dragonfly behavior, this creature remained in the immediate area for nearly thirty minutes, occasionally hovering directly in front of him as if making eye contact.

The next evening, the dragonfly returned, exhibiting the same unusual behavior. David began to see this as his grandfather's way of encouraging him to embrace change and trust in his ability to navigate new directions. Drawing inspiration from the dragonfly's mastery of movement in all dimensions, David found the courage to submit his resignation and begin his teaching career.

The Dragonfly's Message of Adaptability

Dr. Swart's neuroplasticity research provides fascinating insight into why dragonfly encounters often coincide with periods of major life transitions. During times of change, our brains are actively forming new neural pathways and releasing old patterns—a process that mirrors the dragonfly's ability to shift directions instantly. The appearance of these adaptable creatures during transitional periods may represent our subconscious recognition of our own capacity for change and growth.

Dragonflies spend most of their life cycle underwater as nymphs before transforming into aerial beings capable of extraordinary flight maneuvers. This dramatic transformation from water to air, from limitation to freedom, resonates deeply with those facing major life changes or grieving the loss of loved ones. Their message often relates to trusting the process of transformation, even when we cannot see the final outcome.

Feathers: Whispers from Angels

Among all winged messengers, feathers may be the most subtle yet profound signs from beyond. Their appearance in unexpected places—indoors, on clean pathways, or in locations where birds rarely venture—often feels like gentle calling cards from angels, spirit guides, or deceased loved ones announcing their presence.

Feathers carry rich symbolic meaning across cultures. In ancient Egyptian mythology, the goddess Ma'at weighed hearts against her feather of truth to determine the soul's worthiness for the afterlife. Celtic traditions viewed feathers as channels of celestial communication, while many Indigenous cultures consider them sacred objects connecting earth and sky, physical and spiritual realms.

Colors and Their Meanings

White feathers are most commonly associated with angelic presence, representing purity, peace, and divine protection. Their discovery often brings immediate comfort to those struggling with grief or fear, serving as gentle reminders that spiritual support surrounds them.

Gray feathers may indicate a period of neutrality or balance, suggesting the importance of remaining calm during uncertain times. They often appear when we need to maintain equilibrium between different aspects of our lives or decisions.

Brown feathers connect us to earth energy and grounding, often appearing when we need to focus on practical matters while maintaining spiritual awareness. They may signal the importance of stability and home connections.

Black feathers, rather than being ominous, often represent protection and the absorption of negative energy. They may appear during difficult periods as assurance that we are being shielded from harmful influences.

Linda's Pillow Messages

For Linda, feathers became a consistent form of communication from her daughter Sarah, who passed away in a car accident at age nineteen. Beginning about a month after Sarah's death, Linda began finding single white feathers in impossible locations—on her pillow when she woke, inside her purse, on her car dashboard after it had been parked in a covered garage.

What made these discoveries particularly meaningful was their timing. The feathers appeared during Linda's most difficult emotional moments: before

28

Sarah's birthday, on the anniversary of the accident, and whenever Linda questioned whether she could continue living without her daughter. Each feather felt like Sarah's way of saying, "I'm still here, Mom. You're going to be okay."

From Dr. Swart's perspective, Linda's heightened emotional state during grief made her RAS exceptionally sensitive to unusual occurrences. Her brain, seeking comfort and connection, recognized these feather appearances as meaningful rather than coincidental. However, the consistent indoor locations and precise timing of these discoveries created a pattern that suggested intentional placement beyond normal environmental factors.

The Healing Power of Recognition

What makes winged messengers so powerful in the healing process is their ability to transform our perspective from loss to connection, from despair to hope. Dr. Swart's research on neuroplasticity shows that each time we recognize and acknowledge a meaningful sign, we strengthen neural pathways associated with comfort, hope, and spiritual connection.

The act of noticing these messengers creates what neuroscientists call "positive neuroplasticity"—the brain's tendency to focus on and remember uplifting experiences. Over time, this attention to meaningful signs literally rewires our neural architecture to be more receptive to comfort and less focused on despair.

Creating a Messenger Journal

To enhance your ability to recognize and benefit from winged messengers, consider keeping a dedicated journal for these encounters. Record:

- **Date and time** of the sighting
- **Your emotional state** before the encounter
- **Specific behaviors** you observed (unusual duration, fearlessness, direct approaches)
- **Your immediate feelings** during and after the encounter
- **Life circumstances** or decisions you were contemplating
- **Any intuitive messages** you received

Over time, patterns may emerge that reveal your personal symbolic language with winged messengers. You might notice that cardinals appear during family-related concerns, butterflies during periods of major change, or dragonflies when you need encouragement to adapt to new circumstances.

Scientific Wonder and Spiritual Meaning

The remarkable abilities of these winged messengers add to their mystique as spiritual communicators. Cardinals can live up to fifteen years and have excellent memory, potentially explaining their ability to recognize and return to specific locations. Monarch butterflies navigate thousands of miles using magnetic fields and genetic memory, suggesting extraordinary sensitivity to forces beyond ordinary perception. Dragonflies have nearly 360-degree vision and can see polarized light patterns invisible to humans, giving them awareness of dimensions we cannot perceive.

Rather than diminishing their spiritual significance, understanding these natural abilities enhances our appreciation for how divine intelligence might work through creation's existing systems. As Dr. Swart notes, recognizing the neuroscience behind spiritual experiences doesn't negate their meaning—it reveals the elegant ways our brains and spirits collaborate to create healing and connection.

Practical Guidelines for Recognition

To enhance your receptivity to winged messengers while maintaining healthy discernment:

- **Stay Present:** Winged messengers often appear during quiet, mindful moments rather than periods of distraction or rushing.
- **Notice Unusual Behavior:** Pay attention to creatures that linger longer than typical, approach closer than normal, or appear in unexpected locations.
- **Consider Timing:** Messages often coincide with anniversaries, difficult decisions, or moments of particular emotional need.
- **Trust Your Heart:** Authentic encounters typically bring a sense of peace, comfort, or clarity rather than anxiety or confusion.
- **Maintain Balance:** While remaining open to signs, continue engaging fully in practical life responsibilities and relationships.
- **Honor the Message:** Whether through gratitude, journaling, or sharing with trusted friends, acknowledge the comfort these encounters provide.

The Language of Love

Winged messengers remind us that love finds ways to transcend every boundary, including death itself. Through cardinals that visit at precisely the right moments, butterflies that dance through our darkest hours, dragonflies that guide us through transitions, and feathers that appear as gentle calling cards, our departed loved ones continue to participate in our healing journey.

Dr. Swart's neuroscientific framework helps us understand that recognizing these signs isn't wishful thinking but represents the sophisticated ways our brains process meaningful patterns during times of loss and transition. This understanding doesn't diminish the mystery of spiritual communication—it illuminates how science and spirit work together to facilitate healing and maintain the bonds of love that death cannot break.

CHAPTER 4: MESSAGES FROM DEPARTED LOVED ONES

"Death ends a life, not a relationship." — Mitch Albom

"Love is the bridge between two hearts." — Rumi

John sat in his garden six months after losing his wife Sarah, surrounded by the roses she had planted and tended with such devotion. The silence felt overwhelming—no more morning conversations over coffee, no shared observations about the changing seasons, no gentle presence that had anchored his life for thirty-seven years. He found himself speaking aloud to her memory, asking for any sign that love continues beyond death, when something extraordinary happened.

A blue morpho butterfly—a species native to Central and South America and completely foreign to his Midwest location—landed on the bench beside him and remained there for nearly ten minutes. This wasn't just unusual; it was virtually impossible. The butterfly's iridescent wings caught the afternoon light as it seemed to study his face with gentle recognition.

As John later discovered, the blue morpho butterfly was Sarah's favorite creature from their visits to the natural history museum. She had always marveled at their ethereal beauty and often spoke of them as symbols of transformation and hope. The appearance of this impossible messenger in his backyard garden, thousands of miles from its natural habitat, marked the beginning of John's understanding that love finds ways to transcend even death itself.

Dr. Tara Swart's research on the Reticular Activating System helps explain how John's grief-altered brain became exceptionally receptive to meaningful patterns and unusual occurrences. His RAS, focused intensely on seeking connection with Sarah, recognized this butterfly encounter as profoundly significant rather than merely strange. Yet the sheer impossibility of the event— a tropical butterfly appearing in the wrong climate and geographic region—

suggests dimensions of communication that extend beyond neurological pattern recognition.

The Spectrum of After-Death Communication

Messages from departed loved ones manifest through a wide spectrum of experiences, from subtle synchronicities to profound direct encounters. Dr. Swart's neurological research provides crucial insight into why these communications feel so authentic and transformative, while the consistency of reports across cultures and individuals suggests that consciousness may indeed continue beyond physical death.

Modern grief research recognizes after-death communication (ADC) as a common and often healing component of the bereavement process. Rather than pathologizing these experiences or dismissing them as wishful thinking, contemporary psychology acknowledges their potential therapeutic value while encouraging discernment between authentic communication and grief-induced projection.

Direct Sensory Experiences

Many people report sensing the presence of departed loved ones through familiar scents—a mother's perfume lingering in an empty room, the smell of a father's pipe tobacco, or the aroma of a grandmother's cooking appearing without any physical source. These olfactory messages often occur during emotionally significant moments, providing comfort during anniversaries, holidays, or particularly difficult days.

From a neurological perspective, the olfactory system has direct connections to brain regions associated with memory and emotion, making scent-based communications particularly vivid and emotionally resonant. Dr. Swart's research suggests that grief may heighten our sensitivity to subtle environmental changes, including trace scents that might normally go unnoticed.

Electrical and Technological Communication

In our digital age, many people report receiving messages through technological means—flickering lights, phones ringing with no caller, radios playing significant songs, or electronic devices behaving unusually during emotionally charged moments. While skeptics might attribute these to random malfunctions, the timing and context of these events often create meaning that transcends coincidence.

Dr. Swart's understanding of consciousness and energy suggests that strong emotional states may influence electromagnetic fields in ways we don't fully understand. The grieving brain, operating in a heightened state of awareness, may be more sensitive to electromagnetic fluctuations that could influence electronic devices.

Dreams and Sleep State Communications

Dreams provide one of the most commonly reported channels for after-death communication. Unlike ordinary dreams, visitation dreams typically feel more vivid and realistic, leaving dreamers with a profound sense of having genuinely encountered their departed loved one rather than merely dreaming about them.

These dream communications often provide comfort, closure, or guidance about practical matters. Departed parents might offer encouragement during difficult decisions, spouses might share final words of love, or grandparents might provide wisdom about family situations. The emotional healing that results from these dream encounters often validates their authenticity for the dreamer.

Neurologically, REM sleep represents a state of heightened brain activity where normal filtering mechanisms are relaxed, potentially allowing access to information and experiences not available during waking consciousness. Dr. Swart's research suggests that the grieving brain may be particularly receptive to these expanded states of awareness.

Case Study: Margaret's Healing Journey

Margaret's story illustrates how recognizing authentic messages from departed loved ones can facilitate healthy grief processing rather than preventing necessary emotional work. After losing her adult son Michael in a motorcycle accident, Margaret initially experienced typical grief symptoms— intense sadness, disrupted sleep, and difficulty concentrating on daily tasks.

About two months after Michael's death, Margaret began noticing unusual occurrences that seemed to carry his personality and sense of humor. His favorite song played unexpectedly on the radio during her worst emotional moments. Lights flickered in patterns that reminded her of the Morse code he had taught her as a child. Most remarkably, she began finding coins—always pennies, always heads up—in locations where Michael used to leave small surprises for her.

Rather than preventing her from processing grief, these experiences provided comfort that allowed Margaret to face her loss more directly. The messages didn't promise that everything would be easy, but they offered reassurance that Michael's love continued beyond death. This ongoing connection gave her strength to engage in grief counseling, reconnect with friends, and gradually rebuild meaning in her life.

Dr. Swart's neuroplasticity research explains how acknowledging these meaningful connections literally rewired Margaret's brain to focus on love and continuation rather than only loss and finality. Each time she recognized one of Michael's messages and responded with gratitude rather than dismissal, she strengthened neural pathways associated with hope and connection.

Distinguishing Authentic Messages from Grief Projection

Learning to distinguish genuine after-death communication from grief-induced wishful thinking requires developing both openness and discernment. Dr. Swart's research provides scientific frameworks for evaluation, while the wisdom of experienced grief counselors offers practical guidelines for healthy interpretation.

Characteristics of Authentic Communication

Genuine messages from departed loved ones typically share several characteristics that distinguish them from mental projection or coincidental events:

- **Personal Relevance:** Authentic communications often contain specific details, references, or characteristics that reflect the departed person's personality, interests, or relationship with the recipient. Generic or vague experiences are less likely to represent genuine contact.
- **Timing Significance:** Real messages frequently occur during emotionally meaningful moments—anniversaries, birthdays, holidays, or times of particular need or decision-making. Random timing suggests coincidence rather than intentional communication.

- **Emotional Quality:** Authentic encounters typically bring feelings of peace, love, comfort, or gentle guidance rather than anxiety, fear, or pressure to take dramatic action. Departed loved ones seem to communicate in ways that support healing rather than creating additional distress.

- **Behavioral Consistency:** Genuine messages often reflect the departed person's characteristic ways of showing love, providing support, or communicating during their physical lifetime. A practical father might continue offering guidance through meaningful coincidences, while a playful child might communicate through surprising or humorous events.

- **Multiple Witnesses:** When others independently observe or experience the same unusual phenomena, it strengthens the case for authentic communication rather than personal projection. John's blue morpho butterfly, for example, was witnessed by neighbors who confirmed its unusual appearance and behavior.

- **Healing Impact:** Authentic after-death communication typically facilitates healthy grief processing rather than preventing necessary emotional work. Messages that encourage avoiding reality or abandoning practical responsibilities likely represent wishful thinking rather than genuine guidance.

The Neuroscience of Grief and Heightened Perception

Dr. Swart's research reveals that grief creates specific changes in brain chemistry and function that may enhance our ability to perceive subtle environmental changes and meaningful patterns. Rather than representing psychological disturbance, this heightened sensitivity may be an adaptive mechanism that helps us detect sources of comfort and guidance during vulnerable periods.

Neurochemical Changes During Grief

The intense stress of loss triggers significant changes in neurotransmitter production and regulation. Elevated cortisol levels increase alertness and environmental scanning, while disrupted sleep patterns alter normal consciousness states. These neurochemical changes create conditions that may enhance perception of subtle phenomena normally filtered out of awareness.

The grief-altered brain also shows increased activity in regions associated with attachment and social connection, suggesting that our neurological systems remain actively engaged in maintaining bonds with lost loved ones even after physical separation.

The Default Mode Network in Grief

Recent neuroscience research has identified the default mode network (DMN) as particularly active during grief processing. This network, associated with self-referential thinking and internal awareness, may facilitate access to information and experiences not available through normal outward-focused consciousness.

Dr. Swart's work suggests that the grieving DMN may become temporarily more permeable to subtle environmental information, creating opportunities for genuine after-death communication to occur. This enhanced permeability typically decreases as acute grief symptoms subside and normal brain chemistry is restored.

Integration with Professional Support

Understanding the neuroscience of grief-related experiences helps distinguish between healthy spiritual awareness and concerning psychological symptoms. While recognizing potential messages from departed loved ones can support healing, persistent or distressing experiences that interfere with daily functioning require professional evaluation and support.

Mental health professionals increasingly recognize that healthy grief processing can include spiritual experiences without indicating pathology. The key lies in maintaining engagement with practical life responsibilities while remaining open to comfort and guidance from continuing bonds with departed loved ones.

Common Forms of Communication

While each person's experience with after-death communication is unique, certain patterns appear consistently across different cultures, age groups, and belief systems. Understanding these common forms can help individuals recognize potential messages while maintaining appropriate discernment.

Anniversary Phenomena

Many people report increased spiritual activity around anniversaries of their loved ones' deaths, birthdays, or other significant dates. These anniversary phenomena might include unusual dreams, meaningful coincidences, or encounters with significant symbols during emotionally charged time periods.

Dr. Swart's RAS research explains why our brains become hypervigilant during anniversary periods, scanning for meaningful patterns that might provide comfort or connection. The combination of emotional intensity and focused attention creates optimal conditions for recognizing authentic communications when they occur.

Intervention Messages

Sometimes departed loved ones seem to communicate urgent warnings or guidance about safety, health, or important life decisions. These intervention messages often arrive through dramatic dreams, strong intuitive impressions, or unmistakable synchronicities that demand attention and action.

While maintaining healthy skepticism about dramatic claims, several well-documented cases suggest that consciousness may indeed continue beyond death and maintain concern for the welfare of living family members. These communications often provide practical guidance that proves beneficial when followed with appropriate discernment.

Comfort During Transition

Many hospice workers and healthcare professionals report observing deathbed visitations where dying patients appear to communicate with deceased family members or spiritual beings. These experiences often bring profound peace to dying individuals and can provide comfort to grieving families.

While skeptics might attribute these experiences to medication effects or oxygen deprivation, the consistency of reports and their healing impact suggest they may represent genuine spiritual phenomena that ease the transition from physical to spiritual existence.

Guidance Through Difficult Periods

After-death communication often intensifies during periods of major life transitions, health challenges, or family crises. Departed parents might guide their adult children through difficult decisions, deceased spouses might provide encouragement during health challenges, or departed children might offer comfort to grieving siblings.

These guidance communications typically arrive through dreams, meaningful coincidences, or intuitive insights that provide practical wisdom while maintaining emotional connection. The guidance often reflects the departed person's personality and characteristic ways of showing love and support.

Healthy Integration of After-Death Communication

Learning to work with potential messages from departed loved ones requires balancing openness to spiritual experience with engagement in practical healing work. Dr. Swart's research suggests that this integration can enhance rather than hinder healthy grief processing when approached with appropriate discernment.

Maintaining Practical Responsibilities

Authentic spiritual communication typically encourages continued engagement with life rather than escape from reality. Messages that suggest abandoning responsibilities, avoiding professional help, or making impulsive major decisions may represent wish fulfillment rather than genuine guidance.

Healthy integration involves receiving comfort and guidance from continuing spiritual connections while maintaining attention to practical needs, professional relationships, and ongoing healing work. The goal is expanded awareness rather than the replacement of rational thinking.

Professional Support and Spiritual Experience

Mental health professionals increasingly recognize that spiritual experiences can complement rather than complicate therapeutic grief work. Many therapists now receive training in working with clients who report after-death communication, helping them integrate these experiences within a framework of healthy grief processing and emotional healing.

The key is maintaining balance between honoring meaningful spiritual experiences and addressing the practical aspects of grief recovery—rebuilding daily routines, processing complex emotions, and gradually reinvesting in life and relationships. Professional support can help distinguish between a healthy spiritual connection and concerning symptoms that require additional intervention.

Creating Boundaries and Guidelines

Establishing healthy boundaries around after-death communication prevents these experiences from becoming obsessive or interfering with necessary life tasks. Useful guidelines include:

- **Scheduled Connection Time:** Rather than waiting constantly for signs, many people find it helpful to establish regular times for quiet reflection and openness to communication, while maintaining normal awareness during daily activities.

- **Documentation Without Obsession:** Keeping a simple journal of meaningful experiences provides validation without creating pressure to interpret every unusual occurrence as a spiritual message.

- **Community Support:** Sharing experiences with trusted friends, family members, or support groups can provide perspective while avoiding isolation or eccentric interpretations.

- **Professional Consultation:** Regular check-ins with grief counselors or spiritual directors help maintain a healthy perspective while processing the meaning of spiritual experiences within the broader context of healing and growth.

John's blue morpho butterfly, Margaret's meaningful coins, and the countless other examples of after-death communication all point to a profound truth that transcends cultural and religious boundaries: love creates bonds that death cannot sever. Whether understood through Dr. Swart's neuroscientific framework, ancient spiritual wisdom, or simply personal experience, these communications offer healing and hope during life's most challenging transitions.

The key to working with after-death communication lies not in proving or disproving their objective reality, but in receiving their comfort and guidance with appropriate discernment while continuing to engage fully with life, healing, and growth. These experiences remind us that death ends physical presence but not the love, wisdom, and connection that define our most important relationships.

As we learn to recognize and interpret these gentle messages from beyond, we discover that grief need not be a journey into isolation but can become a pathway to expanded awareness and deeper understanding of love's eternal nature.

CHAPTER 5: NATURE'S HEALING MESSENGERS

"Look deep into nature, and then you will understand everything better." — Albert Einstein

"Nature does not hurry, yet everything is accomplished." — Lao Tzu

Emma had been walking the same forest trail for fifteen years, but she had never noticed the hawks. Not until the week after her mother's funeral, when a magnificent red-tailed hawk began appearing at the exact spot where the path curved toward the old oak tree. Day after day, the bird would be perched there as Emma approached, watching her with what seemed like gentle recognition before soaring overhead in wide, graceful circles.

Emma's mother had been a passionate birder, and red-tailed hawks were among her favorite raptors. "They're messengers," her mother used to say during their nature walks together. "They see the big picture from high above and remind us to trust the larger patterns of life." At the time, Emma had dismissed this as her mother's whimsical way of finding meaning in ordinary wildlife encounters.

But now, in her grief, the hawk's consistent presence felt like something more than coincidence. The bird appeared during her most difficult emotional moments—when she questioned her ability to handle her mother's estate, when she struggled with loneliness, when she wondered if she could find meaning in life without her mother's wisdom and guidance. Each time, the hawk's soaring flight seemed to lift her perspective, reminding her that life's challenges looked different from a higher vantage point.

Dr. Tara Swart's research on the Reticular Activating System provides insight into why Emma's grief-altered consciousness became so attuned to this particular wildlife messenger. Her RAS, focused on seeking comfort and connection with her mother's memory, began filtering her environment for experiences that might provide guidance and healing. The hawk's behavior— consistent timing, direct eye contact, and unusual tolerance of human presence—created patterns her brain recognized as meaningful rather than random.

Yet the healing Emma experienced through these encounters suggested dimensions beyond simple pattern recognition. Each hawk sighting brought a sense of peace and perspective that helped her navigate the practical and emotional challenges of grief. Rather than being mere projection of her need for comfort, these experiences seemed to offer genuine guidance about finding balance between honoring her mother's memory and building her own independent life.

The Intelligence of Natural Systems

Modern ecological science reveals that natural systems operate through forms of intelligence and communication that extend far beyond what we typically recognize as consciousness. Trees communicate through underground fungal networks, sharing nutrients and warning signals across forest communities. Plants respond to environmental changes with sophisticated chemical messaging systems. Animals demonstrate navigation abilities that suggest sensitivity to magnetic fields, electromagnetic patterns, and other subtle environmental information.

Dr. Swart's neurological research shows that spending time in nature literally changes our brain chemistry, reducing stress hormones and activating neural networks associated with calm awareness and expanded perspective. This neurological shift creates optimal conditions for receiving both the healing benefits of natural environments and potentially subtle communications from natural systems themselves.

Indigenous wisdom traditions have long understood nature as a living intelligence capable of providing guidance, healing, and spiritual connection. Modern environmental science increasingly validates this perspective, revealing complex communication networks and cooperative relationships that suggest natural systems operate as integrated, responsive communities rather than collections of separate organisms.

Forest Bathing and Neurological Healing

The Japanese practice of shinrin-yoku (forest bathing) has been scientifically validated as a powerful tool for stress reduction and immune system enhancement. Research shows that spending mindful time in forest environments reduces cortisol levels, lowers blood pressure, and increases natural killer cell activity—all factors that support both physical health and emotional resilience during difficult periods.

Dr. Swart's work on neuroplasticity suggests that regular nature contact literally rewires our brains to be more receptive to subtle environmental cues and more capable of the expanded awareness that facilitates recognition of meaningful patterns and potential messages from natural systems.

For those grieving or seeking guidance, this enhanced sensitivity may open channels of communication with natural intelligence that operate below the threshold of ordinary awareness. The healing that results from these nature connections often feels like receiving guidance from a vast, caring intelligence that operates through the natural world itself.

Animal Messengers Beyond Winged Creatures

While cardinals, butterflies, and other winged messengers hold special significance, the natural world offers guidance through countless other animal encounters that arrive with meaningful timing and unusual behavior patterns.

Land Animals as Spiritual Messengers

Deer frequently appear as messengers during times requiring gentleness, intuition, and careful listening. Their silent movement through forest environments and heightened sensitivity to danger make them symbols of intuitive awareness and the ability to navigate challenging terrain with grace.

Marcus's Deer Guidance

During a particularly difficult period in his marriage, Marcus began encountering deer on his early morning runs through suburban neighborhoods—an unusual occurrence in his urban environment. The deer would appear at decision points along his route, standing calmly as he approached before moving deliberately in directions that seemed to guide his path.

These encounters coincided with Marcus's internal struggles about whether to pursue marriage counseling or separation. The deer's peaceful presence and gentle guidance seemed to encourage patience and careful listening—qualities his relationship desperately needed. Following their subtle directional cues during his runs, Marcus discovered new routes that led him to a neighborhood counseling center he hadn't known existed.

Dr. Swart's understanding of the RAS explains how Marcus's brain, focused on seeking guidance about his relationship, became attuned to deer behavior in ways that provided practical direction. Yet the animals' unusual urban appearances and their consistent guidance toward helpful resources suggested a dimension of natural intelligence responding to his need for healing and wisdom.

Rabbits and Cycles of Renewal

Rabbits often appear as messengers during times requiring fertility, creativity, and trust in natural cycles of renewal. Their prolific reproduction and ability to thrive in diverse environments make them symbols of abundance and the potential for new beginnings even in challenging circumstances.

Foxes and Adaptability

Fox encounters frequently coincide with situations requiring cunning, adaptability, and the ability to see through deception or confusion. Their intelligence and versatility in different environments make them guides for navigating complex social or professional situations.

Bears and Inner Strength

Bear sightings, though less common, often signal the need to access inner strength, protective instincts, or the wisdom gained through periods of withdrawal and introspection. The bear's hibernation cycle makes it a powerful symbol of renewal through rest and internal processing.

Weather Patterns as Divine Communication

Natural weather phenomena often carry profound symbolic meaning, arriving with timing that transcends meteorological coincidence to offer guidance, comfort, or confirmation during emotionally significant moments.

Rainbow Messages

Rainbows appearing during funerals, memorial services, or anniversary dates provide some of the most commonly reported and emotionally powerful natural signs. Their sudden appearance after storms creates powerful metaphors for hope emerging from difficult circumstances and the beauty that can follow life's most challenging periods.

Lisa's Wedding Rainbow

Lisa was devastated when her father passed away three weeks before her wedding day. During the outdoor ceremony, as she struggled with his absence during what should have been one of life's happiest moments, storm clouds that had threatened rain all day suddenly parted, revealing a complete double rainbow that arched over the entire wedding party.

The timing was so precise and the rainbow so vivid that even the most skeptical guests interpreted it as her father's way of blessing the marriage and assuring his continued presence in her life. The rainbow's appearance transformed what had been a ceremony shadowed by grief into a celebration that honored both love and loss, presence and remembrance.

Dr. Swart's research on emotional states and environmental sensitivity suggests that intense feelings may heighten our awareness of atmospheric changes that create optimal conditions for rainbow formation. Yet the precise timing of many rainbow experiences during emotionally significant moments suggests possible correlations between consciousness and weather patterns that science hasn't fully explored.

Storm and Clearing Patterns

Sudden storms followed by clearing skies often appear during periods of emotional turbulence, providing natural metaphors for the necessity of processing difficult emotions before achieving clarity and peace. These weather patterns can offer reassurance that current difficulties are temporary and that clarity will emerge from confusion.

Wind Messages

Unusual wind patterns—sudden breezes on still days, wind chimes ringing without apparent cause, or the distinctive sound of wind through specific trees—often provide subtle but meaningful communications during quiet moments of reflection or decision-making.

The movement of wind through natural environments creates ever-changing symphonies of sound that can feel like voices offering encouragement, warning, or guidance. Many people report that paying attention to wind patterns during meditation or contemplative walks provides access to wisdom that transcends ordinary thinking.

Plant and Tree Wisdom

The plant kingdom offers perhaps the most subtle but consistent forms of natural guidance, communicating through growth patterns, flowering cycles, and the healing properties of specific species that seem to appear precisely when their particular medicine is needed.

Flowering Messages

Unexpected flowering—plants blooming out of season, flowers appearing in unusual locations, or specific species thriving despite unfavorable conditions—often carries symbolic meaning about resilience, beauty emerging from difficulty, and the importance of maintaining hope during challenging periods.

Rose's Memorial Garden

After losing her teenage daughter in a car accident, Rose created a memorial garden featuring flowers that had special meaning in their relationship. The garden struggled initially, with many plants failing to thrive despite Rose's careful attention and ideal growing conditions.

On the first anniversary of her daughter's death, Rose discovered that the garden had suddenly burst into spectacular bloom overnight—flowers that had shown no signs of budding the day before were in full flower, creating a display of color and beauty that took her breath away. Neighbors confirmed that the transformation had occurred between evening and morning, making it impossible to explain through normal horticultural processes.

The garden's sudden flowering marked a turning point in Rose's grief journey, providing tangible evidence of beauty and renewal emerging from the deepest sorrow. The flowers' miraculous appearance gave her permission to begin healing while honoring her daughter's memory through the ongoing care of this living memorial.

Tree Messages and Forest Wisdom

Ancient trees, with their deep roots and long lifespans, often serve as symbols of stability, endurance, and the wisdom gained through surviving countless seasons of change. Many people report receiving guidance through encounters with particularly impressive or unusually located trees.

The practice of tree meditation—sitting quietly with a tree and opening to its presence and energy—provides access to what many experience as ancient wisdom about patience, resilience, and the importance of deep roots during life's storms. This practice, validated by research showing measurable physiological benefits from tree contact, offers both stress reduction and potential access to natural intelligence.

Sacred Groves and Power Places

Certain natural locations seem to concentrate healing energy and spiritual communication in ways that transcend their objective environmental characteristics. These power places—sacred groves, ancient forests, distinctive rock formations, or particularly beautiful natural settings—often serve as portals for profound spiritual experiences and meaningful guidance.

Indigenous traditions worldwide recognize specific locations as having special spiritual significance, places where the veil between physical and spiritual realms becomes thinner and communication with natural intelligence flows more easily. Modern visitors to these locations often report heightened intuitive awareness and meaningful encounters with natural messengers.

Water as Healing Messenger

Water's flow patterns, sounds, and reflective qualities make it one of nature's most powerful healing messengers, offering both practical therapy through negative ion generation and symbolic guidance through its constant movement and transformation.

Ocean Messages

Ocean environments provide profound metaphors for the emotional processing required during grief and healing. Wave patterns—their constant motion, the rhythm of approaching and receding, the way they reshape shorelines over time—mirror the natural flow of emotions and the gradual transformation that occurs through healthy grief work.

Many people report receiving guidance through ocean meditation, allowing the rhythm of waves to regulate breathing and emotional states while opening awareness to subtle messages carried on sea breezes and reflected in wave patterns.

River and Stream Guidance

Moving water in rivers and streams offers messages about flow, persistence, and the power of gradual change to overcome seemingly impossible obstacles. The sound of moving water creates natural meditation environments that facilitate access to deeper wisdom and intuitive guidance.

Still Water Reflection

Lakes and ponds provide opportunities for reflection and contemplation, their still surfaces serving as natural mirrors for both physical forms and emotional states. Many contemplative traditions use still water as a focal point for meditation and spiritual inquiry.

The appearance of wildlife around water sources—waterfowl, fish, amphibians—often carries additional symbolic meaning about adaptation, transformation, and the ability to thrive in multiple environments.

Practical Guidelines for Nature Communication

Developing a relationship with natural messengers requires both openness to subtle communication and practical knowledge about wildlife behavior, seasonal patterns, and environmental conditions that might influence animal and plant activities.

Creating Receptive Awareness

Spending regular time in natural environments without electronic devices or distractions creates optimal conditions for recognizing meaningful natural messages. This practice of "nature sitting"—quietly observing natural environments with patient attention—allows subtle patterns and unusual behaviors to become apparent.

Seasonal Sensitivity

Understanding natural seasonal rhythms helps distinguish between ordinary environmental changes and potentially meaningful variations in animal behavior, plant growth, or weather patterns. Unusual animal appearances, out-of-season flowering, or unexpected weather events carry more significance when they deviate from normal seasonal expectations.

Documentation and Pattern Recognition

Keeping a nature journal that records unusual animal encounters, distinctive plant behaviors, and meaningful weather events helps identify patterns that might not be apparent from individual experiences. Over time, these records often reveal sophisticated communication systems operating through natural environments.

Balancing Interpretation with Appreciation

While remaining open to guidance from natural messengers, it's important to maintain appreciation for the intrinsic value and beauty of natural encounters without forcing symbolic interpretation onto every wildlife sighting or environmental event. The healing power of nature often lies simply in its beauty, complexity, and the sense of connection it provides to larger systems of life and meaning.

Integration with Environmental Awareness

Understanding natural messengers enhances rather than conflicts with scientific environmental awareness and ecological responsibility. The recognition that natural systems operate through complex communication and intelligence networks supports rather than contradicts efforts to protect and preserve natural environments.

Dr. Swart's research suggests that the enhanced environmental sensitivity developed through spiritual practice with natural messengers often leads to increased ecological awareness and environmental protection behaviors. People who experience personal guidance and healing through natural encounters typically develop stronger motivation to preserve natural habitats and support environmental conservation efforts.

This integration of spiritual practice with environmental responsibility creates positive feedback loops where personal healing through nature connection motivates broader healing of natural systems, while healthy environments provide enhanced opportunities for meaningful spiritual encounters with natural intelligence.

Emma's relationship with the red-tailed hawk evolved over two years from grief support to environmental advocacy. Her deepening appreciation for the hawk's wisdom led her to volunteer with local raptor conservation programs and support habitat preservation efforts. This evolution from personal healing to community service demonstrates how natural messengers often guide us toward ways of contributing to the healing of both personal and environmental systems.

The hawk continues to appear in Emma's life, though less frequently and more seasonally, as her acute grief has transformed into an ongoing connection with her mother's memory and values. These continued encounters remind her that the natural world offers not just temporary comfort during crisis but an ongoing relationship with intelligence and wisdom that transcends individual human experience.

CHAPTER 6: THE LANGUAGE OF NUMBERS AND DREAMS

"Numbers are the highest degree of knowledge. It is knowledge itself." — Plato

"Dreams are the royal road to the unconscious." — Sigmund Freud

Emma found herself waking at exactly 3:33 AM every night for two weeks following her grandmother's funeral. At first, she attributed this to normal grief-related sleep disruption, but the precision of the timing began to feel significant. Her grandmother had always been fascinated by what she called "angel numbers"—recurring numerical sequences that she believed carried messages from spiritual realms.

During those predawn hours of wakefulness, Emma's mind would flood with vivid memories of her grandmother's stories about numbers and their meanings. Her grandmother had taught her that 333 represented divine protection and the presence of ascended masters offering guidance during difficult transitions. As Emma lay awake night after night at precisely 3:33, she began to feel her grandmother's comforting presence and wisdom surrounding her in the darkness.

Dr. Tara Swart's research on the Reticular Activating System explains how Emma's grief-focused attention made her hyperaware of this specific time pattern. Her RAS, primed by emotional significance and her grandmother's teachings, filtered her consciousness to recognize 3:33 as meaningful rather than coincidental. Yet the consistency of these awakenings, combined with the healing Emma experienced during those quiet hours of reflection and memory, suggested a dimension of communication that transcended simple pattern recognition.

The numerical language that began with 3:33 expanded as Emma's healing progressed. She began noticing meaningful number sequences throughout her day—on receipts, license plates, digital clocks, and addresses—each appearance feeling like a gentle reminder of continued guidance and protection. Rather than becoming obsessive, this awareness brought comfort and a sense of ongoing connection with her grandmother's love and wisdom.

The Mathematics of Meaning: Understanding Angel Numbers

In our digitally saturated world, numerical sequences have become one of the most commonly reported forms of spiritual communication. These "angel numbers"—repetitive or sequential digits that seem to appear with meaningful timing and frequency—provide a bridge between the mathematical precision of universal law and the personal guidance many seek during times of transition or uncertainty.

Dr. Swart's neurological research reveals why numerical patterns carry such psychological impact. Our brains are evolutionarily wired for mathematical thinking, with specific neural networks dedicated to processing numerical relationships and sequential patterns. When we encounter repeating number sequences during emotionally significant moments, multiple brain regions activate simultaneously, creating experiences that feel both intellectually compelling and intuitively meaningful.

The phenomenon of angel numbers operates through the same mechanisms that allow us to recognize faces, detect musical patterns, or navigate complex spatial environments. The RAS, functioning as our consciousness filter, becomes attuned to numerical sequences that align with our current intentions, questions, or emotional needs. This doesn't diminish the spiritual significance of these experiences—it reveals how spiritual guidance works through our natural cognitive abilities rather than bypassing them.

Common Angel Number Sequences and Their Traditional Meanings

- **111 - Manifestation and New Beginnings:** The sequence 111 often appears during periods when our thoughts and intentions carry particular creative power. Its appearance may signal that we're entering a manifestation phase where focused intention can more easily become reality.

- **222 - Balance and Partnership:** This sequence frequently relates to relationships, cooperation, and the need for balance between different aspects of life. It may appear when we need to focus on collaboration, patience, or diplomatic solutions to challenges.

- **333 - Divine Protection and Spiritual Growth:** As Emma experienced, 333 often signals the presence of spiritual guides or ascended masters offering support during challenging transitions. It represents the trinity of mind, body, and spirit working in harmony.

- **444 - Foundation and Stability:** This sequence typically relates to building solid foundations, whether in career, relationships, or spiritual practice. Its appearance often encourages persistence through challenging but necessary work.

- **555 - Change and Transformation:** The appearance of 555 often signals major life changes approaching. Rather than being a warning, it typically serves as encouragement to embrace transformation with confidence and trust.

- **666 - Material and Spiritual Balance:** Contrary to popular misconceptions, 666 in angel number interpretation often relates to the need to balance material concerns with spiritual awareness. It may appear when we're overly focused on financial worries or when we need to address practical matters we've been avoiding.

- **777 - Spiritual Awakening and Inner Wisdom:** This sequence frequently appears during periods of heightened spiritual awareness or when we're being encouraged to trust our inner wisdom over external opinions.

- **888 - Material Abundance and Achievement:** The number 888 often relates to financial improvement, career advancement, or the manifestation of long-term goals. It may appear as encouragement during challenging periods.

- **999 - Completion and Service:** This sequence typically signals the completion of a life phase or the call to serve others through our experiences and wisdom.

- **1111 - Spiritual Portal and Heightened Awareness:** Perhaps the most commonly reported angel number, 1111 often appears during significant spiritual openings or when we're being called to pay particular attention to our thoughts and intentions.

Case Study: David's Numerical Guidance System

David's experience with angel numbers demonstrates how this form of spiritual communication can provide practical guidance while maintaining grounded decision-making. As a financial advisor facing a career transition from corporate banking to independent practice, David was overwhelmed by the complexity of practical and ethical considerations involved in the change.

The numerical guidance began with 555, which appeared consistently during his most intense periods of career uncertainty—on clocks when he was reviewing business plans, on receipts after meetings with potential partners, and on addresses of buildings where he conducted informational interviews. Understanding 555 as encouragement to embrace change, David began moving more confidently toward independent practice.

As his transition progressed, the numerical messages evolved to match his changing needs. During contract negotiations, 444 appeared frequently, encouraging him to focus on building solid foundations rather than rushing toward quick profits. When he worried about financial stability, 888 would appear at precisely relevant moments, reassuring him that his careful planning would yield material abundance.

Dr. Swart's research on neuroplasticity explains how David's consistent attention to these numerical patterns literally rewired his brain to be more confident in decision-making and more trusting of his intuitive business sense. Each time he recognized an angel number and took appropriate action, he strengthened neural pathways associated with self-trust and entrepreneurial confidence.

Three years after his career transition, David's independent practice thrives beyond his original projections. He continues to receive occasional numerical guidance, though less frequently than during the intense transition period. His experience demonstrates how angel numbers can provide practical support during major life changes while encouraging the development of independent judgment and decision-making capabilities.

The Neuroscience of Dream Communication

Dreams represent one of humanity's most ancient and universal forms of spiritual communication, offering a bridge between conscious awareness and deeper dimensions of wisdom and insight. Modern neuroscience reveals that dreaming serves essential functions in memory consolidation, emotional processing, and creative problem-solving, while also potentially providing access to information and guidance that transcends ordinary waking consciousness.

Dr. Swart's research on brain states during sleep shows that REM dreaming involves unique neural activity patterns that differ significantly from both waking consciousness and other sleep stages. During dreams, normal filtering mechanisms are relaxed, logical constraints are suspended, and the brain's pattern-recognition systems operate with enhanced creativity and intuitive connection.

This altered brain state creates optimal conditions for receiving guidance, processing emotional material, and accessing insights that might not be available through linear thinking. The symbolic language of dreams allows complex psychological and spiritual truths to be communicated through images, emotions, and narratives that speak directly to unconscious understanding.

Types of Spiritually Significant Dreams

- **Visitation Dreams:** These dreams involve encounters with deceased loved ones that feel more vivid and emotionally real than ordinary dreams. Visitation dreams often provide comfort, closure, or specific guidance about practical matters. The dreamer typically wakes with a profound sense of having genuinely connected with the departed person rather than simply dreaming about them.

- **Prophetic Dreams:** Some dreams seem to contain information about future events or outcomes that couldn't be logically predicted from available information. While maintaining appropriate skepticism about dramatic predictions, many people report dreams that provided helpful preparation for upcoming challenges or opportunities.

- **Healing Dreams:** These dreams involve experiences of physical, emotional, or spiritual healing that carry over into waking life. They may include encounters with healing figures, symbolic imagery related to recovery, or direct experiences of energy or light that promote healing.

- **Guidance Dreams:** Dreams that provide specific direction about life decisions, creative projects, or relationship matters often contain symbolic or direct guidance that proves helpful when applied with appropriate discernment.

- **Teaching Dreams:** Some dreams involve receiving instruction from wise figures—whether recognized spiritual teachers, deceased mentors, or unknown guides—about spiritual principles, life lessons, or practical skills.

Case Study: Patricia's Dream Healing

Patricia's journey with dream healing began during her recovery from breast cancer treatment. Throughout her chemotherapy, she experienced vivid dreams involving a wise woman who appeared to be conducting healing ceremonies using light, water, and natural elements. These dreams felt profoundly different from ordinary dream experiences—more vivid, emotionally resonant, and memorable.

The dream healer would guide Patricia through elaborate healing rituals involving visualization of light entering her body, immersion in healing waters, and connection with natural environments. Patricia would wake from these dreams feeling physically refreshed and emotionally strengthened, better able to cope with the challenging aspects of cancer treatment.

Dr. Swart's research on neuroplasticity and healing suggests that Patricia's healing dreams may have activated neural networks associated with immune function, stress reduction, and pain management. The vivid imagery and emotional engagement of these dream experiences could have stimulated real physiological changes that supported her recovery process.

Patricia began incorporating elements from her healing dreams into her waking life—visualization practices, therapeutic baths, and time in natural environments. Her medical team noted that she seemed to tolerate treatments better and recover more quickly than many patients with similar diagnoses.

Three years later, Patricia remains cancer-free and continues to receive occasional healing dreams, particularly during times of stress or minor illness. She has trained as a guided imagery facilitator, helping other cancer patients work with visualization and dream practices as complementary healing tools. Her experience demonstrates how dream guidance can provide practical support for physical healing while working in partnership with conventional medical care.

Working with Dream Guidance

Developing a relationship with dream wisdom requires both receptivity to symbolic communication and practical skills for dream recall, interpretation, and integration. Unlike numerical signs that appear in external environments, dream guidance emerges from internal dimensions of consciousness that require different approaches for recognition and understanding.

Dream Recall Enhancement

Improving dream recall creates the foundation for working with dream guidance. Practical techniques include:

- **Intention Setting:** Before sleep, explicitly request dreams that provide guidance, healing, or connection with spiritual wisdom. This programming helps direct unconscious attention toward meaningful dream content.

- **Dream Journal:** Keep a journal beside your bed and record dreams immediately upon waking, before moving or engaging with daily activities. Even fragments or emotional impressions provide valuable information.

- **Sleep Hygiene:** Maintaining consistent sleep schedules, avoiding screens before bedtime, and creating peaceful sleep environments support the deep sleep states that produce meaningful dreams.

- **Gradual Awakening:** When possible, allow yourself to wake naturally rather than using jarring alarms. Gentle awakening preserves dream memories that harsh interruptions can erase.

Symbol Dictionary Development

Personal dream symbols often differ from universal interpretations found in dream dictionaries. Developing your own symbol vocabulary based on personal associations and experiences provides more accurate guidance than generic interpretations.

- **Water:** May represent emotions, unconscious material, purification, or spiritual cleansing, but personal associations with specific bodies of water add individual meaning layers.

- **Animals:** Often represent instinctual wisdom, particular qualities (courage, gentleness, cunning), or messages from spiritual guides, but personal relationships with specific animals influence interpretation.

- **Flying:** Typically represents freedom, transcendence, or the ability to rise above current circumstances, but your personal associations with flight experiences influence specific meaning.
- **Houses:** Often symbolize different aspects of the self or psyche, with various rooms representing different psychological states or life areas.
- **Deceased Loved Ones:** Appearances by departed family members or friends usually provide comfort, guidance, or closure, but the nature of your relationship with the person affects the dream's meaning.

Integration Practices

Working with dream guidance effectively requires translating symbolic insights into practical application while maintaining appropriate discernment about dramatic or unusual dream content.

- **Morning Reflection:** Spend time immediately after waking reflecting on dream emotions, imagery, and any sense of guidance or direction received. Often, the feeling-tone of a dream provides more valuable information than specific symbolic details.
- **Creative Expression:** Drawing, painting, or writing about significant dreams helps integrate their symbolic content and often reveals additional layers of meaning not apparent during initial recall.
- **Dialogue Techniques:** Many dream workers find value in imagining conversations with dream figures or symbols, asking for clarification or additional guidance about unclear dream elements.
- **Action Steps:** When dreams seem to offer practical guidance, consider small experimental steps rather than dramatic life changes. Dream wisdom often works best when integrated gradually with waking consciousness and practical considerations.

The Science of Synchronicity in Numbers and Dreams

Dr. Swart's research provides crucial frameworks for understanding how both numerical synchronicities and meaningful dreams operate through natural brain processes while potentially accessing information beyond ordinary consciousness. Rather than viewing scientific and spiritual explanations as contradictory, her work suggests they represent different levels of understanding the same phenomena.

Neurological Basis of Pattern Recognition

The brain's pattern recognition systems evolved to detect meaningful relationships that could affect survival—predator movements, seasonal changes, social dynamics, and environmental threats or opportunities. These same neural networks now operate in complex modern environments, scanning for patterns that might provide guidance, safety, or advantage.

When we're facing uncertainty, stress, or major life transitions, these pattern recognition systems become hyperactivated, making us more sensitive to numerical sequences, symbolic coincidences, and dream imagery that might provide direction or comfort. This heightened sensitivity doesn't create meaningful patterns—it helps us notice genuine synchronicities that might otherwise escape attention.

The Role of Emotional States

Strong emotional states—whether from grief, love, fear, or excitement—significantly influence both RAS filtering and dream content. During emotionally charged periods, our brains become more receptive to information that relates to current concerns and more likely to retain memories of meaningful coincidences or symbolic dreams.

Dr. Swart's research shows that emotional intensity literally changes brain chemistry in ways that enhance memory formation, pattern recognition, and intuitive processing. This explains why meaningful numbers and dreams often cluster around periods of loss, transition, or major life decisions—times when emotional activation creates optimal conditions for recognizing and remembering significant patterns.

Integration Guidelines: Balancing Openness with Discernment

Working effectively with numerical and dream guidance requires developing sophisticated discernment skills that honor both spiritual openness and practical wisdom. Dr. Swart's research provides valuable frameworks for distinguishing between meaningful synchronicities and random coincidences, authentic dream guidance, and psychological projection.

Evaluating Angel Number Experiences

Meaningful numerical synchronicities typically share certain characteristics that distinguish them from random pattern recognition:

- **Emotional Resonance:** Authentic angel number experiences usually produce immediate feelings of recognition, peace, or clarity rather than anxiety or confusion. The body's response often provides more reliable information than mental analysis.

- **Contextual Relevance:** Genuine numerical messages typically relate directly to current life circumstances, decisions, or emotional states rather than appearing during random moments without personal significance.

- **Practical Application:** Real spiritual guidance usually supports wise decision-making and positive life choices rather than encouraging escapism or abandonment of responsibilities.

- **Consistency Without Obsession:** Meaningful number patterns appear naturally without creating compulsive behavior or interfering with daily functioning. Healthy spiritual awareness enhances life rather than dominating it.

- **Integration with Other Guidance:** Authentic angel numbers typically align with guidance received through other channels—intuition, trusted advisors, practical considerations—rather than contradicting all other sources of wisdom.

Assessing Dream Guidance

Distinguishing meaningful dreams from ordinary psychological processing requires attention to several factors:

- **Vividness and Recall:** Spiritually significant dreams often feel more vivid and are more easily remembered than ordinary dreams.

They may wake you up or leave lasting impressions that persist throughout the day.

- **Emotional Impact:** Meaningful dreams typically produce emotional responses that feel different from regular dream emotions—more peaceful, healing, or clarifying rather than anxious or chaotic.
- **Symbolic Consistency:** Authentic dream guidance often uses symbols that relate to your personal history, relationships, or spiritual practice rather than generic or culturally programmed imagery.
- **Practical Relevance:** Genuine dream guidance usually relates to current life circumstances or provides insight that proves helpful when applied with appropriate discernment.
- **Healing Effect:** Meaningful dreams typically promote emotional healing, relationship improvement, or spiritual growth rather than increasing fear, guilt, or confusion.

Case Study: Jennifer's Integrated Guidance System

Jennifer's experience demonstrates how numerical and dream guidance can work together to provide comprehensive support during major life transitions. As a teacher considering whether to pursue a master's degree in counseling, Jennifer was overwhelmed by the practical complexities and emotional uncertainty involved in changing careers at age forty-five.

The guidance began with consistent appearances of 555, which she interpreted as encouragement to embrace change. These numerical signs appeared during her most intense periods of career uncertainty, providing reassurance that transformation was not only possible but necessary for her growth.

The numerical guidance was complemented by a series of dreams featuring her deceased mentor, Mrs. Chen, who had encouraged Jennifer's interest in counseling during her undergraduate years. In these dreams, Mrs. Chen would guide Jennifer through symbolic scenarios representing different aspects of counseling work—listening to troubled individuals, providing comfort during crisis, and creating safe spaces for healing.

Dr. Swart's research explains how Jennifer's brain, focused on career transition concerns, became attuned to both numerical patterns and dream content that related to her decision-making process. Her RAS filtered environmental information to highlight 555 sequences while her dreaming mind processed career anxieties through symbolic encounters with trusted guidance figures.

Rather than making decisions based solely on spiritual signs, Jennifer used these experiences as sources of encouragement while conducting practical research about counseling programs, speaking with professionals in the field, and assessing her financial readiness for a career change. The combination of spiritual support and practical preparation gave her confidence to apply for graduate school and begin her transition.

Three years later, Jennifer has completed her counseling degree and established a successful private practice specializing in grief counseling. She continues to receive occasional numerical guidance and meaningful dreams, though less frequently than during her intense transition period. Her experience demonstrates how spiritual guidance can provide emotional support and direction while working in partnership with practical decision-making and professional preparation.

The intersection of numerical synchronicity and dream guidance with modern neuroscience reveals how ancient wisdom practices and contemporary understanding can enhance each other. Dr. Swart's research validates what contemplative traditions have long understood: consistent spiritual practice literally changes brain structure in ways that enhance our capacity for meaningful pattern recognition and symbolic interpretation.

Understanding these brain changes doesn't reduce spiritual experience to mere neural activity—it reveals how spiritual practices optimize our neurological capacity to receive guidance from deeper dimensions of consciousness and reality. Rather than explaining away mystery, science helps us appreciate the sophisticated ways consciousness interfaces with universal intelligence to provide guidance during our times of greatest need.

CHAPTER 7: DEVELOPING YOUR SPIRITUAL ANTENNA

"Be still and know that I am God." — Psalm 46:10

"The quieter you become, the more you are able to hear." — Rumi

Rachel had always been skeptical of meditation. As a busy emergency room physician, her world revolved around quick decisions, immediate action, and tangible results. The idea of sitting quietly and "doing nothing" felt like an impossible luxury and a potential waste of precious time. But after losing two patients in one particularly difficult week—deaths that she couldn't prevent despite her best medical efforts—Rachel found herself questioning everything she thought she knew about healing, consciousness, and the limits of scientific medicine.

A colleague suggested she try a brief meditation practice to help process the stress and emotional toll of her work. Reluctantly, Rachel began with just five minutes each morning, sitting in her car before entering the hospital. At first, her mind raced with patient cases, treatment protocols, and endless to-do lists. But gradually, something began to shift.

After several weeks of consistent practice, Rachel noticed she was becoming more aware of subtle cues in her work environment—changes in patients' conditions that she couldn't quite explain through standard medical assessment, intuitive hunches about treatment approaches that proved surprisingly effective, and moments of knowing that seemed to transcend her medical training.

Dr. Tara Swart's research on meditation and brain function helps explain Rachel's experience. Regular meditation practice literally rewires neural pathways, enhancing our capacity for present-moment awareness, pattern recognition, and what neuroscientists call "interoceptive sensitivity"—the ability to perceive subtle internal and environmental cues that normally operate below the threshold of conscious awareness.

Most remarkably, Rachel began experiencing what she could only describe as spiritual guidance during particularly challenging medical situations. In moments of quiet focus during procedures or patient interactions, she would receive clear impressions about treatment approaches, communication strategies with families, or simply the sense of presence that seemed to provide comfort to both patients and herself.

This development of what Rachel came to call her "spiritual antenna" didn't compromise her medical expertise—it enhanced it. Her colleagues began noticing her increased effectiveness with difficult cases and her seemingly intuitive ability to provide exactly the right support to families during crisis situations.

The Neuroscience of Contemplative Awareness

Dr. Swart's groundbreaking research reveals that meditation and contemplative practices create measurable changes in brain structure and function that enhance our capacity for spiritual awareness. These changes aren't merely subjective experiences—they represent actual neurological developments that can be observed through brain imaging and measured through cognitive and emotional assessments.

Regular meditation practice increases gray matter density in brain regions associated with attention, self-awareness, and compassion while reducing activity in areas linked to stress, anxiety, and self-centered thinking. These structural changes create optimal conditions for the kind of expanded awareness that facilitates recognition of spiritual signs and subtle guidance.

The Default Mode Network and Spiritual Awareness

One of Dr. Swart's most significant discoveries relates to meditation's impact on the Default Mode Network (DMN)—a network of brain regions active during rest and introspection. In most people, the DMN generates constant mental chatter, self-referential thinking, and what contemplatives call "monkey mind"—the endless stream of thoughts that prevents deeper awareness.

Meditation practice gradually quiets DMN activity while strengthening neural networks associated with present-moment awareness and focused attention. This neurological shift creates what many meditators describe as "spaciousness"—a quality of consciousness that allows subtle spiritual impressions to emerge without being drowned out by mental noise.

This spaciousness represents the foundation of spiritual antenna development. When the mind becomes quiet and receptive, we naturally become more sensitive to the subtle signs, synchronicities, and intuitive guidance that constantly surround us but typically remain unnoticed in our busy, distracted states of consciousness.

Neuroplasticity and Spiritual Development

Dr. Swart's research on neuroplasticity reveals that spiritual antenna development isn't limited by age, previous experience, or innate abilities. The brain remains capable of forming new neural connections and developing enhanced sensitivity to subtle information throughout our lives.

Each time we practice meditation, notice a meaningful synchronicity, or act on intuitive guidance, we strengthen neural pathways that support spiritual awareness. This process creates positive feedback loops where spiritual practice enhances our capacity for spiritual experience, which in turn motivates continued practice and development.

Essential Practices for Developing Spiritual Sensitivity

The development of spiritual sensitivity requires consistent practice with techniques that quiet mental chatter while enhancing present-moment awareness. Unlike developing physical skills, spiritual antenna cultivation involves learning to receive rather than do, to listen rather than speak, to be rather than achieve.

Breath Awareness Meditation

The simplest and most fundamental practice involves focusing attention on the natural rhythm of breathing. This anchors consciousness in the present moment while providing a reliable object of focus that's always available.

Basic Technique:
- Sit comfortably with spine erect but not rigid
- Close eyes or soften gaze downward
- Notice the natural flow of breath without controlling it
- When the mind wanders, gently return attention to breathing
- Start with 5-10 minutes daily and gradually extend duration

Dr. Swart's research shows that even brief breath awareness practice begins changing brain activity patterns within weeks, creating the neurological foundation for enhanced spiritual sensitivity.

Body Scanning Practice

This technique develops what neuroscientists call interoceptive awareness—sensitivity to internal bodily sensations that often carry intuitive information before it reaches conscious thought.

Progressive Body Awareness:

- Lie down comfortably or sit with good posture
- Begin at the top of the head, slowly moving attention through each part of the body
- Notice sensations without trying to change anything
- Pay particular attention to areas that feel tense, warm, cool, or energized
- Complete the scan from head to toes, then rest in whole-body awareness

Many practitioners discover that body scanning reveals subtle energy patterns and sensations that correlate with spiritual guidance and environmental information.

Open Awareness Practice

This advanced technique involves maintaining receptive attention to all arising experiences without focusing on any particular object. It develops the kind of spacious awareness that facilitates recognition of spiritual signs and synchronicities.

Choiceless Awareness Technique:

- Sit quietly with eyes closed or soft gaze
- Instead of focusing on breath or other objects, remain open to whatever arises in consciousness
- Notice thoughts, sensations, sounds, and emotions without engaging with their content
- Maintain the perspective of witnessing awareness rather than identifying with particular experiences
- Rest in the space of awareness itself rather than its contents

This practice requires some foundation in basic meditation but develops the receptive quality that characterizes spiritual sensitivity.

Creating Sacred Space for Practice

The environment where we practice meditation and contemplative awareness significantly influences our capacity to develop spiritual sensitivity. While formal meditation doesn't require elaborate settings, thoughtful attention to our practice space enhances both the quality of our sessions and our ongoing receptivity to spiritual guidance.

Physical Environment Considerations

Choose a location that feels peaceful and won't be disturbed during practice sessions. This might be a corner of a bedroom, a spot in a garden, or even a consistent place in your car if home privacy isn't available. The key is regularity—using the same location builds energetic familiarity that supports deeper states of awareness.

Minimize distractions by turning off electronic devices, choosing times when others are less likely to interrupt, and creating visual calm through simple, uncluttered surroundings. Natural elements—plants, stones, water features—often enhance the meditative atmosphere without requiring elaborate arrangements.

Energetic Preparation

Many traditions recognize that spaces accumulate the energy of activities performed there. Regular meditation and prayer gradually imbue locations with peaceful vibrations that support continued practice. This explains why established meditation spaces often feel immediately calming to sensitive individuals.

Simple rituals like lighting candles, burning incense, or offering brief prayers help shift consciousness from daily concerns to contemplative awareness. These preparatory activities signal to both the conscious and unconscious mind that this time and space are dedicated to spiritual receptivity.

Time and Consistency

Dr. Swart's neuroplasticity research emphasizes that consistency creates more profound brain changes than duration. Daily fifteen-minute sessions produce better results than weekly hour-long practices. The brain responds to repeated patterns, building stronger neural pathways through regular reinforcement.

Many practitioners find that early morning sessions, before daily activities begin, offer optimal conditions for spiritual antenna development. The mind is naturally quieter upon awakening, and morning practice establishes a foundation of centered awareness that influences the entire day.

Intermediate Practices: Deepening Receptivity

As basic meditation skills develop, intermediate practices can enhance specific aspects of spiritual sensitivity while maintaining the grounded awareness that prevents spiritual bypassing or disconnection from practical responsibilities.

Loving-Kindness Meditation

This practice develops emotional openness and heart-centered awareness that facilitates reception of guidance motivated by love and compassion rather than fear or ego desires.

Heart-Opening Technique:

- Begin with basic breath awareness to establish calm attention
- Bring to mind someone you love easily and naturally
- Generate feelings of warmth, appreciation, and well-wishing toward this person
- Extend similar feelings toward yourself, using phrases like "May I be happy, may I be peaceful"
- Gradually include neutral people, difficult people, and all beings in expanding circles of loving intention
- Rest in the open-hearted awareness that results from this practice

Research shows that loving-kindness meditation increases activity in brain regions associated with empathy and emotional regulation while reducing stress and defensive reactivity.

Nature Connection Practice

Spending contemplative time in natural environments enhances our sensitivity to the subtle communication systems that operate through the living world. Natural settings provide both the negative ions that support nervous system regulation and the complex sensory environments that develop perceptual sensitivity.

Outdoor Meditation Approach:

- Find a natural location where you can sit quietly without disturbance
- Begin with breath awareness to establish present-moment attention
- Gradually expand awareness to include sounds, smells, visual patterns, and air movement
- Notice the quality of attention that emerges when consciousness includes rather than excludes environmental information
- Pay attention to any sense of communication or guidance that emerges through natural phenomena

Many practitioners report that regular nature meditation develops their capacity to receive guidance through animal appearances, weather patterns, and plant behaviors that feel meaningfully timed and personally relevant.

Contemplative Reading and Reflection

Working with spiritual texts, poetry, or wisdom teachings through contemplative reading develops our capacity to receive guidance through written words and symbolic communication.

Lectio Divina Approach:

- Choose a brief spiritual passage or meaningful text
- Read slowly several times, paying attention to words or phrases that capture your attention
- Sit quietly with these highlighted words, allowing them to rest in consciousness without analysis
- Notice any insights, images, or guidance that emerges through this receptive engagement
- Conclude with gratitude for any wisdom received

This practice bridges reading and meditation, developing our ability to receive spiritual guidance through the written word while maintaining the receptive awareness that characterizes spiritual sensitivity.

Advanced Techniques: Expanding Awareness

As spiritual antenna development progresses, advanced practices can deepen our capacity for subtle perception while maintaining integration with daily life and practical responsibilities.

Intuitive Journaling

This practice involves writing from receptive awareness rather than analytical thinking, allowing guidance and insights to emerge through spontaneous expression.

Stream-of-Consciousness Writing:

- Set aside 15-20 minutes with pen and paper or computer
- Begin with a question or area where you're seeking guidance
- Write continuously without stopping to edit, analyze, or correct
- Allow whatever emerges to flow onto paper without judging its value or accuracy
- Review your writing later with discerning attention to insights that feel authentic and helpful

Many practitioners discover that intuitive journaling accesses wisdom and perspective that wasn't available through normal thinking processes.

Energy Sensing Practice

Developing sensitivity to subtle energy patterns enhances our ability to receive information through non-verbal channels and environmental changes.

Basic Energy Awareness:

- Sit quietly with hands resting on knees or in lap
- Slowly bring palms toward each other without touching
- Notice any sensations between your hands—warmth, tingling, pressure, or movement
- Experiment with expanding and contracting this field of sensation
- Practice sensing the energy of different people, places, or objects with patient, non-judgmental attention

While maintaining healthy skepticism about dramatic energy claims, many people develop reliable sensitivity to subtle environmental information through this practice.

Contemplative Movement

Practices like walking meditation, yoga, or tai chi integrate physical movement with contemplative awareness, developing embodied sensitivity that includes both physical and spiritual dimensions.

Walking Meditation Technique:

- Choose a quiet path 10-20 steps long
- Walk very slowly, paying attention to each component of movement

- At the end of your path, pause and turn mindfully
- Continue walking back and forth, maintaining present-moment attention to movement and surroundings
- Notice how this quality of attention affects your sensitivity to environmental information and internal guidance

Movement practices often reveal how spiritual sensitivity includes bodily wisdom and how physical and spiritual awareness integrate naturally when developed together.

Case Study: Marcus's Transformative Practice

Marcus's journey with spiritual antenna development demonstrates how consistent practice can transform both personal effectiveness and capacity for service. As a social worker dealing with challenging family situations, Marcus initially approached meditation as stress management rather than a spiritual practice.

His daily twenty-minute morning sessions gradually developed into something more profound than relaxation. Marcus began noticing subtle cues in his work environment—changes in family dynamics that weren't obvious through standard assessment, intuitive hunches about which interventions might be most helpful, and moments of knowing that seemed to transcend his professional training.

Dr. Swart's research explains how Marcus's meditation practice enhanced his capacity for pattern recognition and emotional sensitivity—skills directly applicable to his social work practice. The same neural changes that support spiritual awareness also enhance professional effectiveness in fields requiring high levels of interpersonal sensitivity.

Most significantly, Marcus began receiving what he could only describe as guidance during particularly challenging cases. In moments of quiet focus during family meetings or case planning, he would receive clear impressions about communication approaches, resource connections, or intervention strategies that proved remarkably effective.

This development of spiritual sensitivity didn't compromise Marcus's professional standards—it enhanced them. His supervisors noted his increased effectiveness with difficult cases and his seeming ability to find exactly the right resources for families in crisis.

Three years after beginning meditation practice, Marcus leads mindfulness groups for social workers and trains colleagues in contemplative approaches to human services. His experience demonstrates how spiritual antenna development can enhance rather than conflict with professional excellence and ethical service.

Integration with Daily Life

The ultimate goal of spiritual antenna development isn't to achieve special states of consciousness but to integrate expanded awareness with ordinary life activities. This integration allows spiritual sensitivity to enhance rather than replace practical effectiveness and relational engagement.

Mindful Transitions

Developing the habit of brief centering practices during daily transitions— between meetings, before meals, when arriving home—maintains the receptive awareness cultivated during formal practice while engaging fully with practical responsibilities.

Brief Centering Practice:

- Take three conscious breaths before beginning new activities
- Set clear intentions about bringing presence and awareness to upcoming tasks
- Notice one thing you're grateful for in your current environment
- Proceed with activities while maintaining some background awareness of breath and bodily sensation

These micro-practices maintain spiritual sensitivity without requiring additional time or special conditions.

Relational Awareness

Applying contemplative attention to relationships and conversations develops our capacity to receive guidance about communication, emotional support, and conflict resolution.

Contemplative Listening:

- During conversations, maintain some attention on your breath and bodily sensations
- Listen not just to words but to emotional undertones and unspoken concerns
- Notice your own reactive impulses without immediately acting on them

- Remain open to insights about helpful responses that emerge from receptive awareness rather than defensive thinking

Many people discover that contemplative listening enhances their ability to provide exactly the kind of support others need while reducing interpersonal stress and conflict.

Decision-Making Integration

Incorporating spiritual sensitivity into decision-making processes provides access to wisdom that transcends logical analysis while maintaining appropriate use of rational thinking and practical considerations.

Integrated Decision Process:

- Gather relevant practical information through normal research and consultation
- Spend quiet time with the decision, asking for guidance and remaining open to insights
- Notice your body's response to different options—expansion or contraction, energy or depletion
- Consider how different choices align with your values and contribute to the welfare of others
- Make decisions that integrate practical wisdom, intuitive guidance, and ethical considerations

This approach honors both spiritual sensitivity and practical responsibility, creating decisions that serve both personal growth and community welfare.

Maintaining Balance and Perspective

Developing spiritual sensitivity requires maintaining balance between openness to subtle guidance and engagement with practical responsibilities. Dr. Swart's research emphasizes that healthy spiritual development enhances rather than replaces rational thinking, emotional intelligence, and social engagement.

Avoiding Spiritual Bypassing

The term "spiritual bypassing" describes the tendency to use spiritual practices or beliefs to avoid dealing with practical responsibilities, difficult emotions, or necessary psychological work. Healthy spiritual antenna development includes rather than excludes engagement with the full spectrum of human experience.

Authentic spiritual guidance typically supports rather than contradicts sound judgment, ethical behavior, and compassionate engagement with others' needs. Guidance that encourages escape from reality, abandonment of responsibilities, or grandiose self-importance likely represents ego projection rather than genuine spiritual communication.

Professional Support Integration

Spiritual antenna development can complement but should never replace appropriate professional support when dealing with serious mental health concerns, medical issues, or major life crises. The goal is expanded awareness that enhances our capacity to work effectively with qualified professionals rather than spiritual practices that substitute for necessary practical intervention.

Many mental health professionals now recognize that contemplative practices can support therapeutic work by developing self-awareness, emotional regulation, and access to inner resources. The key is maintaining both spiritual openness and practical engagement with evidence-based approaches to healing and growth.

Community and Relationship Integration

Healthy spiritual development enhances rather than replaces our capacity for meaningful relationships and community engagement. Spiritual sensitivity should increase our ability to serve others effectively rather than creating isolation or spiritual superiority.

Rachel's experience in emergency medicine demonstrates this integration perfectly. Her spiritual antenna development enhanced her medical effectiveness and her ability to provide compassionate care during crisis situations. Her colleagues sought her consultation not because she had become otherworldly, but because her combination of medical expertise and spiritual sensitivity made her an unusually effective healer and colleague.

Conclusion: The Ongoing Journey

Developing spiritual sensitivity represents an ongoing journey rather than a destination to be reached. Like physical fitness or artistic skill, spiritual antenna development requires consistent practice, patience with the natural rhythms of growth, and integration with the other dimensions of healthy human development.

Dr. Swart's research validates what contemplative traditions have long understood: regular spiritual practice creates measurable changes in brain structure and function that enhance our capacity for wisdom, compassion, and service. These changes support rather than conflict with practical effectiveness, emotional intelligence, and social engagement when spiritual development is approached with appropriate balance and perspective.

As we continue developing our spiritual antenna, we discover that the ability to receive guidance and healing from spiritual dimensions represents our natural birthright rather than a special gift available only to a few. Through patient practice and integration, we can all develop the receptive awareness that allows us to participate consciously in the ongoing dialogue between human consciousness and the vast intelligence that pervades all existence.

CHAPTER 8: DIVINE TIMING AND SYNCHRONICITY

"There is a time for everything, and a season for every activity under the heavens." — Ecclesiastes 3:1

"Synchronicity is an ever-present reality for those who have eyes to see." — Carl Jung

Alexandra stood at the crossroads of her life, literally and figuratively. After fifteen years as a corporate marketing executive, she had reached a point where success felt hollow and the demands of her career were taking an unsustainable toll on her health and relationships. She dreamed of opening a small wellness center that would combine her business skills with her passion for holistic healing, but the financial risks seemed overwhelming.

The synchronicities began on a Tuesday morning in March. While contemplating whether to submit her resignation, Alexandra received an unexpected call from a former colleague who mentioned that the perfect building for a wellness center had just become available in her neighborhood— at below-market rent. That afternoon, her accountant called with surprising news about a forgotten investment that had matured, providing exactly the seed money she needed for her business venture.

By Friday of that same week, three different people had independently referred clients who were seeking the exact type of integrated wellness services Alexandra envisioned offering. The convergence of these events felt too precisely orchestrated to be mere coincidence, yet Alexandra's analytical mind struggled to accept that such perfect timing could represent anything beyond random chance.

Dr. Tara Swart's research on the Reticular Activating System provides a partial explanation for Alexandra's experience. When we focus intensely on specific goals or decisions, our RAS begins filtering environmental information to highlight opportunities and resources that align with our intentions. This neurological mechanism helps explain why synchronicities often cluster around periods of major life transitions or significant decision-making.

Yet the precision and emotional resonance of Alexandra's synchronicities suggested dimensions beyond simple pattern recognition. The timing felt guided by an intelligence that understood not just her conscious desires but also her deeper spiritual needs and readiness for transformation. This intersection of personal intention with seemingly cosmic orchestration characterizes what many experience as divine timing.

Understanding the Mechanics of Divine Timing

Divine timing operates at the intersection of personal intention, spiritual readiness, and the mysterious coordination of external events that seems to support our highest good. Unlike human timing, which focuses on efficiency and immediate results, divine timing appears to consider factors we cannot perceive—the readiness of other people, the alignment of circumstances, and our own spiritual preparation for receiving what we've requested.

Dr. Swart's research reveals that during periods of intense focus and emotional significance, our brains become exceptionally sensitive to environmental patterns and meaningful coincidences. This heightened awareness creates optimal conditions for recognizing synchronistic events that might otherwise escape our notice. However, the consistency and precision of many synchronistic experiences suggest that consciousness may participate in information fields that extend beyond individual neural networks.

The Paradox of Effort and Surrender

Divine timing often requires a delicate balance between focused intention and relaxed receptivity. Too much forcing or urgent pushing can actually block the natural flow of synchronistic support, while complete passivity may fail to engage the creative collaboration between human intention and divine intelligence.

Alexandra's experience illustrates this paradox perfectly. Her intense desire for a career change created the emotional activation necessary for her RAS to recognize relevant opportunities, but her willingness to remain open to unexpected possibilities allowed the synchronicities to unfold naturally rather than being forced into preconceived patterns.

Recognizing Divine Timing Patterns

Authentic divine timing typically shares certain characteristics that distinguish it from random coincidence or forced interpretation of ordinary events:

- **Convergence of Multiple Factors:** Divine timing often involves the simultaneous alignment of several different elements—opportunities, resources, connections, and circumstances—that individually might seem unrelated but together create optimal conditions for progress or transformation.

- **Emotional Resonance:** Synchronistic events aligned with divine timing typically produce feelings of recognition, gratitude, or peaceful excitement rather than anxiety or confusion. The body's response often provides more reliable information than mental analysis about whether particular coincidences represent meaningful guidance.

- **Perfect Practicality:** Divine timing frequently manifests through completely practical means—job opportunities, financial resources, helpful connections, or timely information—rather than dramatic supernatural events. The divine intelligence seems to work through natural processes rather than bypassing them.

- **Developmental Appropriateness:** Authentic divine timing supports genuine growth and development rather than gratifying ego desires or enabling escapism. The opportunities and resources that appear through synchronicity typically match our actual readiness and capacity rather than our fantasies or fears.

- **Service Orientation:** Divine timing often includes elements that serve not just personal needs but also the welfare of others or the larger community. Synchronistic events frequently create opportunities for mutual benefit rather than purely selfish advancement.

The Neuroscience of Meaningful Coincidence

Dr. Swart's research provides fascinating insights into the neurological mechanisms that support our recognition and interpretation of synchronistic events. Rather than dismissing meaningful coincidences as mere projection or wishful thinking, her work reveals how our brains are sophisticated instruments for detecting genuine patterns and significant timing in our environment.

Pattern Recognition and Emotional Significance

The human brain contains specialized neural networks dedicated to recognizing patterns, predicting outcomes, and detecting meaningful relationships between apparently separate events. During emotionally significant periods—times of crisis, transition, or intense focus—these pattern recognition systems become hyperactivated, making us more sensitive to environmental information that relates to our current concerns.

This heightened sensitivity doesn't create meaningful patterns—it enhances our ability to notice genuine synchronicities that might normally escape conscious awareness. The key distinction lies in emotional resonance: authentic synchronicities typically produce immediate feelings of recognition or significance that transcend intellectual analysis.

The Role of Intention in Synchronicity

Dr. Swart's work on the RAS demonstrates how clearly focused intentions program our consciousness to notice information and opportunities that align with our goals. This programming effect helps explain why synchronicities often increase in frequency and precision when we become clear about what we truly desire or need.

However, intention setting for synchronicity requires a specific quality of focus—one that combines clarity about desired outcomes with openness to unexpected forms of manifestation. Rigid attachment to specific methods or timing often blocks the natural flow of synchronistic support, while vague or conflicted intentions provide insufficient direction for the RAS to filter relevant information effectively.

Neuroplasticity and Synchronicity Recognition

Regular attention to synchronistic experiences literally rewires our brains to become more sensitive to meaningful patterns and precise timing. Each time we notice a meaningful coincidence and respond with gratitude or appropriate action, we strengthen neural pathways that support continued recognition of divine timing.

This neuroplasticity explains why some people seem naturally attuned to synchronicity while others rarely notice meaningful coincidences. The capacity for synchronicity recognition can be developed through practice and attention, regardless of starting point or previous experience.

Working with Divine Timing: Practical Approaches

Learning to recognize and respond appropriately to divine timing requires developing both receptivity to subtle guidance and discernment about when to act versus when to wait. This balance involves trusting the process while remaining grounded in practical wisdom and ethical responsibility.

Intention Setting for Synchronicity

Effective intention setting creates optimal conditions for divine timing to operate while maintaining the flexibility necessary for unexpected forms of manifestation.

Clear Vision Creation:

- Identify your authentic desires rather than what you think you should want
- Focus on the essential qualities of what you're seeking rather than specific details about how it should manifest
- Include consideration for the welfare of others affected by your intentions
- Remain open to possibilities that exceed your current imagination or understanding
- Release attachment to specific timeframes while maintaining persistent gentle focus

Alexandra's intention-setting process illustrates this approach perfectly. Rather than demanding a specific type of business opportunity by a particular deadline, she focused on her desire to serve others through work that utilized both her business skills and healing interests. This clear but flexible intention created space for synchronicity to operate while providing sufficient direction for her RAS to recognize relevant opportunities.

Developing Synchronicity Sensitivity

Enhancing our ability to recognize meaningful coincidences requires cultivating the same receptive awareness discussed in previous chapters while developing specific attention to timing, patterns, and emotional resonance.

Daily Synchronicity Practice:

- Begin each day with a brief meditation or reflection, setting gentle intentions for guidance and support
- Maintain relaxed awareness throughout daily activities, noticing unusual coincidences or meaningful patterns
- Pay attention to your emotional response to potential synchronicities—authentic events typically produce feelings of recognition or gratitude
- Document meaningful coincidences in a journal, noting timing, emotional context, and any guidance received
- End each day with gratitude for any synchronistic support experienced, regardless of magnitude

Acting on Divine Timing

Responding appropriately to synchronistic guidance requires distinguishing between authentic divine timing and coincidences that carry personal meaning but don't necessarily indicate action steps. This discernment develops through experience and integration with other forms of wisdom and guidance.

Guidelines for Synchronistic Action:

- Consider whether synchronistic events align with your values, long-term goals, and ethical principles
- Assess whether acting on apparent guidance would serve the welfare of others as well as your own development
- Take experimental steps rather than dramatic life changes based solely on synchronistic experiences
- Integrate synchronistic guidance with practical considerations, professional advice, and input from trusted friends or advisors
- Maintain engagement with normal decision-making processes while remaining open to synchronistic support and confirmation

Case Study: Michael's Career Transition

Michael's experience with divine timing demonstrates how synchronicity can guide major life transitions while working in partnership with practical planning and professional development. After twenty years as a high school teacher, Michael felt called to become a therapist but was overwhelmed by the practical challenges of returning to graduate school while supporting his family.

The synchronistic guidance began subtly. Michael repeatedly encountered information about therapy programs during his normal activities—magazine articles in waiting rooms, overheard conversations, online advertisements that seemed precisely targeted to his interests. These coincidences might have been easily dismissed except for their timing and emotional impact.

The informational encounters consistently appeared during Michael's most intense periods of career questioning, often providing exactly the practical information he needed about financing, program requirements, or career prospects. More significantly, each synchronistic event produced feelings of encouragement and clarity rather than anxiety or confusion.

Dr. Swart's research explains how Michael's focused concern about career transition made his RAS exceptionally sensitive to therapy-related information in his environment. His brain, primed by emotional significance and clear intention, began filtering his experience to highlight relevant opportunities and resources.

The synchronicities escalated when Michael finally committed to pursuing therapy training. Within one week of submitting his first application, he received news about scholarship opportunities he hadn't known existed, connected with a mentor who offered exactly the guidance he needed, and learned about a program that would allow him to continue teaching part-time while completing his degree.

Most remarkably, Michael discovered that his teaching position included tuition benefits for graduate programs that his personnel office had never mentioned during his twenty years of employment. The timing of this discovery—one day after he had calculated the financial impossibility of returning to school—felt like direct confirmation that his career transition was supported by forces beyond his individual planning.

Three years later, Michael has completed his therapy degree and established a successful practice specializing in adolescent counseling. His teaching background provides unique qualifications for working with young people and their families, creating a career integration he hadn't anticipated when he first considered the transition.

Michael continues to experience occasional synchronicities related to his practice development, though less frequently than during his intense transition period. His experience demonstrates how divine timing can provide both practical support and emotional encouragement during major life changes while working in partnership with thorough planning and professional preparation.

The Collective Dimension of Synchronicity

Divine timing often operates not just in individual lives but through collective events that seem orchestrated to serve larger purposes or bring together people who need each other's support or collaboration. Understanding this collective dimension helps us recognize how our personal synchronicities may serve broader healing and growth that extends beyond individual benefit.

Community Synchronicity

Many people report experiencing synchronicities that bring them into contact with exactly the right people at precisely the right time for mutual support, collaboration, or shared learning. These community synchronicities often feel guided by intelligence that understands the needs and gifts of multiple individuals simultaneously.

Global Synchronicity Patterns

During periods of collective crisis or transformation, many individuals report increased synchronicity related to similar themes—environmental awareness, social justice, spiritual awakening, or community building. These parallel experiences suggest that divine timing may operate through collective fields of consciousness that coordinate individual awakenings for larger purposes.

Synchronicity and Service

Divine timing frequently guides individuals toward opportunities for service that utilize their unique talents and experiences while addressing community needs. These service synchronicities often feel like being called to contribute to healing or growth that extends beyond personal advancement.

Shadow Aspects: When Timing Feels Wrong

Understanding divine timing requires acknowledging the shadow aspects of synchronicity—periods when meaningful events seem absent, when timing feels frustratingly slow, or when synchronicities appear to guide us toward difficult rather than pleasant experiences.

The Dark Night of Synchronicity

Many people experience periods when meaningful coincidences seem to disappear entirely, leaving them feeling abandoned by the divine intelligence they had come to trust. These dry periods often occur during times of spiritual growth or life transition when previous forms of guidance no longer serve our developmental needs.

Dr. Swart's research suggests that these apparent synchronicity droughts may represent neurological integration periods when the brain is reorganizing neural networks to support new levels of awareness and capability. Rather than indicating abandonment, the absence of obvious guidance may signal that we're developing the internal resources necessary for more independent spiritual functioning.

Challenging Synchronicities

Sometimes divine timing seems to guide us toward difficult experiences—job losses that force career reevaluation, relationship endings that open space for growth, or health challenges that redirect life priorities. These challenging synchronicities often feel meaningful but unwelcome, creating confusion about whether we're receiving guidance or punishment.

Understanding challenging synchronicities requires expanding our perspective about divine timing beyond immediate comfort or convenience. Often, these difficult events prove to be precisely what was needed for spiritual growth, character development, or preparation for future service, even when this larger purpose isn't apparent during the challenging period itself.

Discernment and False Synchronicity

Not every meaningful coincidence represents authentic divine timing. Our pattern-seeking brains can create apparent significance from random events, especially during periods of emotional intensity or desperate need for guidance. Developing discernment about authentic versus projected synchronicity requires attention to several factors:

- **Emotional Quality:** Authentic divine timing typically produces feelings of peace, recognition, or gentle excitement rather than anxiety, desperation, or grandiose inflation.
- **Practical Wisdom:** Genuine synchronicities usually align with sound judgment, ethical principles, and consideration for others'

welfare rather than contradicting practical wisdom or encouraging harmful behavior.

- **Long-term Perspective:** Real divine timing often supports long-term growth and development rather than providing immediate gratification or escape from necessary challenges.
- **Community Impact:** Authentic synchronicity frequently serves not just individual needs but also contributes to community welfare or larger purposes.

Integration with Daily Life

Working effectively with divine timing requires integrating awareness of synchronicity with practical responsibility, professional competence, and healthy relationships. The goal isn't to live entirely through synchronistic guidance but to include divine timing as one source of wisdom among many.

Professional Integration

Alexandra's wellness center venture demonstrates healthy integration of synchronistic guidance with business planning, market research, and professional development. The synchronicities provided encouragement and resources, but Alexandra still conducted thorough planning, obtained proper training, and developed realistic business projections.

This integration creates what might be called "spiritually informed professionalism"—approaches to work and career that remain open to divine timing while maintaining standards of competence, ethics, and service that serve both personal growth and community welfare.

Relationship Balance

Working with divine timing in relationships requires maintaining the balance between openness to synchronistic guidance and respect for others' autonomy and decision-making processes. Synchronicities may provide insights about relationship dynamics or timing, but they shouldn't replace direct communication, mutual consent, or ethical consideration for others' needs and boundaries.

Decision-Making Integration

The most effective approach to divine timing involves using synchronistic experiences as one source of information among many rather than relying exclusively on coincidental guidance for major life decisions. This integration might include:

- Gathering practical information through normal research and consultation
- Paying attention to synchronistic events that relate to current decisions
- Seeking input from trusted advisors and professional consultants
- Considering ethical implications and impact on others
- Making decisions that integrate practical wisdom, synchronistic guidance, and value-based considerations

Advanced Practices: Deepening Divine Partnership

As sensitivity to divine timing develops, advanced practices can deepen our capacity for conscious collaboration with the intelligent forces that seem to orchestrate meaningful events in our lives.

Co-creative Manifestation

This approach involves setting clear intentions while remaining actively receptive to synchronistic guidance about methods, timing, and opportunities for manifestation.

Co-creative Process:

- Clarify your authentic desires and intentions through contemplative reflection
- Release attachment to specific outcomes while maintaining focus on essential qualities
- Take practical steps toward your goals while remaining open to unexpected opportunities
- Pay attention to synchronistic guidance about timing, resources, and collaborative possibilities
- Act on synchronistic opportunities that align with your values and serve broader welfare

Synchronicity Mapping

Advanced practitioners sometimes track patterns of meaningful coincidences over extended periods to understand their personal synchronicity patterns and divine timing cycles.

Pattern Recognition Practice:

- Maintain detailed records of synchronistic experiences over several months or years
- Note correlations between synchronicities and life circumstances, emotional states, or spiritual practices
- Identify recurring themes, symbols, or types of guidance that appear in your synchronistic experiences
- Recognize personal cycles of high and low synchronicity activity
- Use pattern awareness to optimize your receptivity and response to divine timing

Service-Oriented Synchronicity

This advanced practice involves requesting synchronistic guidance specifically for opportunities to serve others or contribute to community welfare rather than focusing primarily on personal needs.

Service Intention Practice:

- Set intentions for guidance about how your unique talents and experiences can serve healing and growth in your community
- Pay attention to synchronicities that bring you into contact with people who need your particular gifts or support
- Notice opportunities for collaboration, mentorship, or community contribution that appear through meaningful coincidences
- Consider how your personal synchronicities might serve larger purposes beyond individual fulfillment

Conclusion: Dancing with Divine Intelligence

Alexandra's wellness center has thrived for three years, serving hundreds of clients while providing her with the meaningful work she had dreamed of during her corporate years. The synchronicities that launched her venture continue occasionally, though less dramatically than during her initial transition. She has learned to recognize divine timing as an ongoing dialogue with intelligent forces that support authentic growth and service when we remain open to their guidance.

Dr. Swart's research provides crucial scientific frameworks for understanding how synchronicity operates through natural brain processes while potentially accessing information and coordination that transcends individual consciousness. This integration of scientific knowledge with spiritual openness creates optimal conditions for recognizing and responding to divine timing when it appears.

The key to working with divine timing lies not in forcing synchronicities or demanding specific outcomes, but in developing the receptive awareness and practical wisdom that allow us to recognize and respond appropriately when meaningful coincidences offer guidance and support. This requires balancing trust in divine intelligence with engagement in practical planning, professional competence, and ethical responsibility.

As we learn to dance with divine timing, we discover that synchronicity represents an ongoing invitation to participate consciously in the larger intelligence that coordinates events for healing, growth, and service. Whether we understand these experiences through neuroscience, spiritual wisdom, or simply appreciation for life's meaningful mysteries, divine timing offers a resource for navigation that can enhance our capacity to serve both personal development and community welfare.

CHAPTER 9: FROM SIGNS TO HEALING ACTION

"Faith without works is dead." — James 2:26

"Be the change you wish to see in the world." — Mahatma Gandhi

Dr. Swart reminds us that noticing signs is only the first step; transformation requires action. Each time we follow an inspired nudge, we strengthen new neural circuits, making it easier to trust our intuition the next time. This is the essence of neuroplasticity in daily life: rewiring the brain to support new habits of awareness, courage, and alignment. By combining signs from the universe with intentional action, we co-create a new reality—one that reflects both divine guidance and the brain's remarkable ability to adapt and grow.

Sarah had been receiving clear signs for months. After her husband's death, meaningful songs played at precisely emotional moments, cardinals appeared during her most difficult days, and the number sequence 444 seemed to follow her everywhere—on clocks, receipts, and license plates. She felt comforted by these messages and grew increasingly confident that her deceased husband was still present in her life. But she also felt stuck.

The signs provided emotional support, but Sarah wasn't sure how to translate their comfort into practical steps forward. She had been a stay-at-home mother for fifteen years, and now faced the daunting prospect of rebuilding her life as a single parent while processing her grief. The spiritual messages reassured her that she wasn't alone, but they didn't pay the bills or help her figure out how to reenter the workforce.

The turning point came when Sarah realized that the signs weren't meant to solve her problems for her—they were meant to give her the confidence and guidance to take healing action herself. Dr. Swart's research on neuroplasticity reveals that spiritual practices and intuitive awareness create optimal brain conditions for creative problem-solving and confident decision-making. The signs weren't replacing her need to act; they were empowering her to act more wisely and courageously.

Sarah began treating each meaningful synchronicity as both comfort and a call to action. When 444 appeared during a difficult conversation with her financial advisor, she interpreted this as encouragement to build a solid foundation—so she enrolled in online courses to update her professional skills. When her husband's favorite song played while she was cleaning out his home office, she took this as guidance to transform that space into a workspace where she could start a freelance consulting business.

The Neuroscience of Inspired Action

Dr. Swart's research reveals that spiritual practices and contemplative awareness create specific changes in brain function that enhance our capacity for wise action. Rather than promoting passivity or wishful thinking, authentic spiritual development actually optimizes the neural networks responsible for decision-making, creative problem-solving, and confident implementation of our goals.

Enhancing Executive Function

Regular meditation and spiritual practice strengthen the prefrontal cortex— the brain region responsible for executive function, planning, and impulse control. This neurological enhancement helps us translate spiritual insights into practical action steps while maintaining the patience and persistence required for meaningful change.

When we receive spiritual guidance—whether through signs, synchronicities, or inner knowing—the strengthened prefrontal cortex helps us evaluate this guidance against practical considerations, ethical principles, and long-term goals. This integration prevents spiritual bypassing while ensuring that our actions remain grounded in both wisdom and effectiveness.

Reducing Fear-Based Reactivity

Spiritual practice also reduces activity in the amygdala, the brain's fear center, while strengthening neural networks associated with calm confidence and emotional regulation. This neurological shift creates optimal conditions for taking inspired action even when external circumstances feel uncertain or challenging.

Sarah's experience illustrates this perfectly. Her consistent attention to spiritual signs gradually reduced her anxiety about the future while increasing her confidence in her ability to navigate practical challenges. The signs didn't eliminate uncertainty, but they provided the emotional stability necessary for taking constructive action despite uncertainty.

Enhancing Creative Problem-Solving

Dr. Swart's research shows that contemplative practices enhance connectivity between different brain regions, particularly areas associated with creativity, insight, and innovative thinking. This enhanced neural communication often leads to creative solutions that wouldn't emerge through logical analysis alone.

Many people report that their most creative and effective solutions emerge during or shortly after spiritual practices—meditation, prayer, nature contemplation, or quiet reflection on meaningful signs. This correlation reflects the brain's enhanced capacity for innovative thinking when the mind is calm, focused, and receptive to new possibilities.

The Decision-Making Trinity: Signs, Logic, and Ethics

Translating spiritual guidance into effective action requires integrating three essential elements: the wisdom received through signs and synchronicities, the practical analysis provided by logical thinking, and the moral compass offered by ethical consideration. Like a three-legged stool, each component provides essential support for wise action.

Signs as Guidance and Encouragement

Spiritual signs function as both directional guidance and emotional encouragement, providing information about potential paths while offering the confidence necessary to pursue challenging or uncertain ventures. However, signs work best when integrated with rather than substituted for practical planning and ethical reflection.

Authentic spiritual guidance typically supports rather than contradicts sound judgment, professional competence, and ethical behavior. When signs seem to encourage actions that violate practical wisdom or moral principles, this usually indicates misinterpretation rather than genuine divine guidance.

Logic as Structure and Safety

Rational analysis provides the practical framework necessary for translating spiritual insights into effective action. This includes assessing feasibility, identifying resources, anticipating challenges, and creating realistic timelines for implementation.

The logical mind also serves as a valuable check against spiritual grandiosity or impulsive decision-making. When spiritual guidance encourages dramatic life changes, logical analysis helps ensure that such changes serve genuine growth rather than escapism or ego inflation.

Ethics as Compass and Integration

Ethical consideration ensures that our inspired actions serve not just personal goals but also the welfare of others and the larger community. This moral dimension often reveals the deeper purpose behind spiritual guidance while preventing actions that might benefit us individually but harm others or violate our values.

Many people discover that their most meaningful and successful inspired actions involve service to others or contribution to community welfare. This correlation suggests that authentic spiritual guidance often includes elements that transcend personal benefit to serve larger purposes.

Case Study: Marcus's Healing Center

Marcus's journey from spiritual signs to practical action demonstrates how this three-part integration can guide major life transitions while serving both personal growth and community healing. After experiencing a series of meaningful synchronicities during his recovery from addiction, Marcus felt called to create a treatment center that integrated conventional recovery methods with spiritual practices.

The signs began during Marcus's early sobriety when he repeatedly encountered information about holistic addiction treatment—magazine articles, conversations, and online resources that appeared with meaningful timing during his most challenging recovery moments. Rather than dismissing these as a coincidence, Marcus began documenting these encounters and reflecting on their potential significance.

Spiritual Guidance

The synchronicities escalated when Marcus began seriously considering whether to pursue training in addiction counseling. Within one week, he received information about scholarship programs, connected with a mentor who had created a successful holistic treatment center, and discovered that his sponsor had been considering similar ideas for their community.

The spiritual guidance provided both direction and encouragement, but Marcus recognized that signs alone weren't sufficient for such a major undertaking. He needed to integrate this guidance with practical planning and ethical consideration.

Practical Analysis

Marcus spent six months researching the addiction treatment field, interviewing professionals, visiting existing centers, and assessing the financial and logistical requirements for starting a new program. This practical analysis revealed both opportunities and challenges that the spiritual signs hadn't addressed directly.

The research phase also helped Marcus understand how his personal recovery experience could contribute to professional effectiveness while identifying areas where he needed additional training and supervision. This realistic assessment prevented grandiose fantasizing while maintaining focus on genuine service.

Ethical Reflection

Throughout his planning process, Marcus remained committed to ensuring that his venture would serve client welfare rather than personal ego or financial gain. He consulted with established professionals, submitted to appropriate oversight, and designed his program according to evidence-based standards rather than purely personal preferences.

This ethical foundation helped Marcus navigate challenges and setbacks during the center's development while maintaining focus on service rather than success. His commitment to client welfare attracted support from other professionals and eventually led to sustainable funding and community recognition.

Integrated Action

Marcus's treatment center has now operated successfully for three years after his initial spiritual signs. The program integrates conventional addiction treatment with mindfulness practices, nature therapy, and spiritual exploration—exactly the combination that his original synchronicities had suggested.

Most importantly, Marcus's approach demonstrates how spiritual guidance can enhance rather than replace professional competence and ethical responsibility. His center maintains high standards for treatment effectiveness while remaining open to the spiritual dimensions of recovery that many clients find essential for lasting sobriety.

Creating Action Plans Guided by Spiritual Wisdom

Developing reliable methods for translating spiritual guidance into effective action requires practical frameworks that honor both spiritual wisdom and pragmatic considerations. These approaches help ensure that our inspired actions serve genuine healing and growth rather than spiritual bypassing or impulsive decision-making.

The Gradual Implementation Model

Rather than making dramatic life changes based on spiritual signs, this approach involves taking small experimental steps that allow for course correction while maintaining stability and responsibility.

Progressive Action Steps:

- Begin with small actions that align with apparent spiritual guidance
- Assess the results of these experimental steps before proceeding further
- Gradually increase commitment and investment as results validate initial guidance
- Maintain flexibility to adjust direction based on outcomes and additional guidance
- Integrate spiritual insights with ongoing practical planning and community input

Sarah's career transition illustrates this model perfectly. Rather than immediately starting a business based on her spiritual signs, she began with skills training, gradual workspace development, and small freelance projects that allowed her to test her guidance while maintaining financial stability.

Living in Sacred Alignment: Creating Your Action Plan Framework

Developing a reliable process for translating spiritual guidance into effective action requires personalized frameworks that honor your unique circumstances, capabilities, and calling while maintaining integration with practical planning and community accountability.

Spiritual Preparation Practices

Before acting on spiritual guidance, establishing a clear connection with your deepest values and intentions creates optimal conditions for wise action.

Contemplative Preparation:

- Regular meditation or prayer practice that quiets mental chatter and enhances receptivity
- Journaling about spiritual experiences and their potential meanings
- Setting clear intentions about serving healing and growth rather than just personal advancement
- Seeking guidance about timing, methods, and community connections that might support your inspired action
- Cultivating gratitude for guidance received while maintaining openness to unexpected forms of manifestation

Practical Planning Integration

Inspired action becomes most effective when spiritual guidance integrates with thorough practical planning rather than replacing it.

Implementation Planning Process:

- Research practical requirements for your inspired action—training, resources, legal considerations, market conditions
- Develop realistic timelines that honor both spiritual timing and practical constraints
- Identify potential obstacles and develop contingency plans
- Seek mentorship from others who have successfully navigated similar transitions or projects

- Create measurement criteria that assess both practical effectiveness and spiritual alignment

Community Accountability Systems

Sharing your inspired action plans with trusted advisors helps maintain both motivation and perspective throughout implementation periods.

Accountability Structures:

- Regular meetings with spiritual mentors, professional advisors, or supportive friends
- Participation in communities of others pursuing inspired action or similar service
- Professional consultation when your action involves specialized skills or community welfare
- Family meetings when your choices significantly affect others' lives
- Periodic review sessions that assess both practical progress and spiritual alignment

Conclusion: The Ripple Effect of Aligned Action

Sarah's freelance consulting business now employs three other single mothers, providing flexible work opportunities for women in similar circumstances while serving clients who value both professional competence and compassionate understanding. What began as personal survival guided by spiritual signs has evolved into service that multiplies healing for others facing similar challenges.

Marcus's treatment center has inspired similar programs in other communities, creating a network of holistic addiction services that integrates spiritual awareness with evidence-based treatment. His willingness to act on spiritual guidance while maintaining professional standards has contributed to broader transformation in addiction treatment approaches.

These stories illustrate the ripple effect of aligned action—the way that following spiritual guidance with practical wisdom creates benefits that extend far beyond individual healing to serve the welfare of entire communities. Dr. Swart's research on neuroplasticity reveals that each time we act on authentic spiritual guidance, we strengthen neural networks that support continued wisdom, courage, and effectiveness in service.

The transformation from receiving signs to taking healing action represents the completion of the spiritual communication cycle. When we learn to receive guidance, interpret it with discernment, and implement it with practical wisdom and ethical responsibility, we become active participants in the ongoing creation of a more healing and conscious world.

Dear Reader,

Thank you so much for choosing *Whispers from Beyond*. I truly hope the stories, guidance, and insights in these pages helped you feel more connected—to the universe, to your intuition, and to the loved ones who continue to walk beside you from beyond.

If this book brought you comfort, clarity, or confirmation in your own spiritual journey, **would you consider leaving an honest review on Amazon?** Your feedback not only supports my work as an independent author, but it also helps other readers who are seeking guidance, healing, and hope to discover this book. Just scan the QR code to review my book.

Your voice has the power to help others find light during their own moments of questioning or loss—and I'm deeply grateful for your time and support.

Thank you for being part of this journey of connection, intuition, and universal wisdom.

With gratitude,
Wendy Samons

CHAPTER 10: LIVING IN SACRED ALIGNMENT

"When you realize there is nothing lacking, the whole world belongs to you." — Lao Tzu

"The privilege of a lifetime is to become who you truly are." — Carl Jung

Three years after beginning my spiritual journey with signs from my deceased son Benjamin, I found myself living a life I couldn't have imagined during my darkest days of grief. What had started as a desperate seeking for any indication that love survives death had evolved into a way of being that integrated spiritual awareness with practical service in ways that felt both natural and transformative.

My morning routine now includes meditation with my coffee as cardinals visit the bird feeder outside my kitchen window—a daily reminder of the ongoing dialogue between my heart and the intelligence that pervades all life. My nursing work has evolved to include supporting families during end-of-life transitions, helping others recognize their own experiences with signs and messages from departing loved ones.

But perhaps most significantly, I have learned to live in what I call "sacred alignment"—a way of being that remains constantly receptive to spiritual guidance while fully engaged with practical responsibilities, professional competence, and loving service to my community. This isn't about achieving some perfect spiritual state, but rather about maintaining the kind of awareness that allows the sacred and mundane to interpenetrate naturally.

Dr. Tara Swart's research provides the neurological framework for understanding how this integrated way of living develops. Consistent spiritual practices literally rewire the brain to maintain the kind of expanded awareness that facilitates ongoing recognition of guidance, meaning, and connection while supporting rather than compromising practical effectiveness and relational engagement.

Sacred alignment doesn't require withdrawing from ordinary life or achieving supernatural abilities. Instead, it involves developing the capacity to remain simultaneously grounded in practical reality and receptive to the spiritual dimensions that provide meaning, guidance, and healing support throughout our daily experience.

The Neurobiology of Integrated Living

Dr. Swart's groundbreaking research reveals that sustained spiritual practice creates measurable changes in brain structure that support what contemplatives have long called "non-dual awareness"—the capacity to remain simultaneously engaged with practical tasks and receptive to spiritual guidance without internal conflict or compartmentalization.

Neural Integration and Whole-Brain Functioning

Regular meditation and contemplative practice enhance communication between different brain regions, particularly connections between areas associated with rational thinking, emotional intelligence, and intuitive awareness. This enhanced neural integration supports the kind of simultaneous functioning that allows spiritual and practical perspectives to inform each other rather than competing for attention.

Unlike compartmentalized thinking that switches between spiritual and practical modes, integrated awareness maintains access to both dimensions simultaneously. This allows inspired action to emerge naturally from the intersection of spiritual guidance and practical wisdom rather than requiring difficult choices between competing perspectives.

The Default Mode Network in Mature Practice

Advanced practitioners often report that the constant mental chatter characterizing ordinary consciousness gradually transforms into what many describe as "dynamic stillness"—a quality of awareness that remains peaceful and spacious while actively engaged with complex tasks and relationships.

Dr. Swart's research shows that this development correlates with specific changes in Default Mode Network activity. Rather than generating endless self-referential thinking, the DMN in experienced practitioners supports what neuroscientists call "meta-cognitive awareness"—the capacity to observe thoughts and emotions while maintaining access to deeper wisdom and perspective.

Neuroplasticity and Sustainable Transformation

Perhaps most importantly, Dr. Swart's work demonstrates that the brain changes supporting sacred alignment become increasingly stable over time. Unlike peak spiritual experiences that fade quickly, consistent practice creates permanent neurological developments that support sustained access to expanded awareness throughout ordinary daily activities.

This neuroplasticity explains how people can maintain spiritual sensitivity while functioning effectively in demanding professional environments. The brain literally develops the capacity to process multiple dimensions of information simultaneously rather than requiring exclusive focus on either spiritual or practical concerns.

Characteristics of Sacred Alignment

Living in sacred alignment manifests through specific qualities and capacities that emerge naturally as spiritual practice matures and integrates with daily life. These characteristics aren't achievements to be pursued directly but rather natural developments that arise when spiritual awareness and practical engagement support each other over time.

Present-Moment Grounding

Sacred alignment involves maintaining primary attention in the present moment while remaining open to guidance, inspiration, and meaning that emerge naturally within immediate experience. This differs from both scattered attention that misses subtle guidance and forced spiritual seeking that overlooks practical reality.

People living in sacred alignment often report that ordinary activities— cooking, working, conversing—become naturally meditative without requiring special effort or technique. The same quality of awareness cultivated during formal meditation extends into all life activities, creating seamless integration between spiritual practice and daily engagement.

Responsive Rather Than Reactive Living

Integrated spiritual awareness develops what psychologists call "response flexibility"—the capacity to pause between stimulus and response, allowing wisdom and compassion to inform our actions rather than reacting automatically from conditioning or emotional impulse.

This responsiveness extends to spiritual guidance as well. Rather than urgently chasing signs or desperately seeking direction, people in sacred alignment remain receptively available to guidance while maintaining patient engagement with whatever life circumstances are currently presenting.

Service as Natural Expression

Perhaps most characteristically, sacred alignment naturally expresses itself through service that utilizes individual gifts for community welfare. This service emerges organically from expanded awareness rather than being imposed through ought or obligation.

My evolution from personal grief work to supporting other families during loss illustrates this natural development. My spiritual awareness enhanced rather than replaced my nursing skills, creating opportunities for service that integrated professional competence with spiritual sensitivity in ways that served both my growth and others' healing.

Sustainable Practices

Sacred alignment develops sustainable approaches to spiritual practice that enhance rather than burden daily life. Rather than requiring extensive retreat periods or elaborate rituals, mature practice integrates spiritual awareness into ordinary activities through brief but consistent practices that maintain connection without creating additional stress.

These might include brief morning meditation, gratitude practices during daily transitions, contemplative walking, or simply maintaining gentle awareness of breath and bodily sensation throughout normal activities. The key is consistency rather than duration, integration rather than separation.

Practical Approaches to Sacred Alignment

Developing sustainable integration of spiritual awareness with daily life requires practical approaches that honor both contemplative development and engagement with ordinary responsibilities. These approaches support gradual transformation rather than dramatic lifestyle changes that might disrupt important relationships or professional obligations.

Daily Practice Integration

Rather than requiring extensive meditation retreats or complex spiritual practices, sacred alignment develops through brief but consistent practices that integrate naturally with daily routines.

Morning Centering Practice:

- Brief meditation or contemplative reading before beginning daily activities
- Setting intentions for remaining receptive to guidance while serving others effectively
- Gratitude practices that acknowledge both practical blessings and spiritual support
- Connection with nature through window gazing, brief outdoor time, or indoor plants

Transition Practices:

- Three conscious breaths between activities or locations
- Brief prayers or intentions when beginning new tasks
- Mindful attention to walking, driving, or other movement between destinations
- Grateful acknowledgment of support received throughout the day

Evening Integration:

- Reflection on meaningful moments, synchronicities, or guidance received during the day
- Gratitude for both practical accomplishments and spiritual experiences
- Brief loving-kindness practice for people encountered throughout the day
- Setting intentions for continued growth and service

Work and Service Integration

Sacred alignment transforms professional and volunteer service by bringing contemplative awareness to ordinary work activities without compromising competence or effectiveness.

Contemplative Work Practices:

- Beginning work periods with brief centering or intention-setting

- Maintaining background awareness of breath and bodily sensation during tasks
- Approaching colleagues and clients with curiosity and compassion rather than judgment
- Seeking opportunities to serve others' development while meeting practical objectives
- Integrating spiritual values with professional ethics and standards

Service as Spiritual Practice:
- Viewing work responsibilities as opportunities for spiritual development
- Bringing full presence and attention to interactions with others
- Looking for ways to contribute to others' welfare within professional roles
- Maintaining awareness of how individual work serves larger community needs
- Balancing personal advancement with contribution to collective welfare

Relationship and Community Integration

Living in sacred alignment enhances rather than replaces engagement with family, friends, and community by bringing greater presence, compassion, and wisdom to relational interactions.

Contemplative Relationships:
- Practicing deep listening that attends to both words and emotional undertones
- Maintaining curiosity about others' perspectives rather than defensive reactivity
- Bringing awareness of spiritual interconnection to daily interactions
- Supporting others' growth while maintaining appropriate boundaries
- Integrating spiritual values with practical relational skills

Community Engagement:
- Participating in community activities that serve collective welfare
- Sharing spiritual insights appropriately without imposing beliefs on others
- Seeking opportunities for service that utilize individual gifts
- Building bridges between spiritual and secular communities
- Contributing to community healing while respecting diverse perspectives

Maintaining Balance and Perspective

Living in sacred alignment requires ongoing attention to maintaining balance between spiritual awareness and practical engagement while avoiding common pitfalls that can undermine healthy integration.

Avoiding Spiritual Bypassing

The most significant danger in sacred alignment involves using spiritual practices or beliefs to avoid dealing with practical responsibilities, difficult emotions, or necessary psychological work.

Healthy sacred alignment includes rather than excludes engagement with practical realities, relational challenges, and personal development work. Spiritual awareness should enhance our capacity to address life's difficulties rather than providing escape from necessary growth work.

Maintaining Professional Competence

Sacred alignment should enhance rather than replace professional skills, ethical standards, and institutional effectiveness. Spiritual insights complement rather than substitute for appropriate training, continuing education, and professional consultation.

My nursing work illustrates this balance perfectly. My spiritual awareness enhanced my ability to support families during difficult transitions, but I maintained all my professional medical standards while seeking appropriate continuing education about grief counseling and end-of-life care.

Community and Relationship Integration

Living in sacred alignment can sometimes create tension with family members or communities that don't understand or share spiritual perspectives. Maintaining important relationships requires sensitivity, respect, and clear communication about changes in perspective while demonstrating continued love and commitment.

The goal is integration rather than conversion—finding ways to honor spiritual development while maintaining connection with important people who may have different approaches to meaning-making and values.

Humility and Continued Learning

Sacred alignment requires maintaining humility about spiritual experiences while remaining open to continued learning and development. This includes willingness to acknowledge mistakes, seek feedback from others, and adjust course when circumstances or understanding change.

Spiritual development never reaches completion, and sacred alignment represents an ongoing process rather than a final achievement. Maintaining beginner's mind and openness to growth prevents spiritual stagnation and supports continued service and effectiveness.

Conclusion: The Ripple Effect of Aligned Living

My integration of spiritual awareness with nursing practice has influenced my entire healthcare workplace. Colleagues increasingly seek my guidance during difficult patient situations, and my supervisor has asked me to mentor new nurses in developing the combination of clinical competence and emotional intelligence that makes me effective with grieving families.

This way of living honors both the mystery of spiritual communication and the practical requirements of contemporary life, creating a sustainable approach to spiritual development that serves healing and transformation at both personal and collective levels. As more people develop this integration, we create possibilities for communities and institutions that operate from expanded awareness while maintaining effectiveness, compassion, and wisdom in addressing the challenges and opportunities of our time.

The signs and messages we've explored throughout this book—from winged messengers to numerical guidance, from synchronicities to dream wisdom—all point toward this fundamental truth: we are constantly surrounded by intelligence and love that seeks to guide us toward our highest good and greatest service. Learning to recognize and respond to this guidance while remaining grounded in practical wisdom creates lives of meaning, purpose, and healing contribution that benefit both ourselves and the communities we serve.

CONCLUSION: THE ONGOING CONVERSATION

"The privilege of a lifetime is to become who you truly are." — Carl Jung

As I sit in my garden this morning, watching the cardinal that still visits my bird feeder three years after Benjamin's death, I'm struck by how profoundly the journey of learning to recognize and interpret universal signs has transformed not just my understanding of death and loss, but my entire approach to living with meaning and purpose.

What began as a desperate seeking for any indication that my son's love survived his physical death has evolved into an ongoing dialogue with the intelligence and compassion that pervades all existence. The signs I've learned to recognize—from winged messengers to numerical sequences, from dream guidance to meaningful synchronicities—have revealed themselves as threads in a vast tapestry of communication that connects us to wisdom, healing, and service opportunities we might otherwise miss.

Dr. Tara Swart's groundbreaking research has provided the scientific framework for understanding how this spiritual communication operates through natural brain processes while potentially accessing information and coordination that transcends individual consciousness. Her work bridges the gap between spiritual experience and scientific understanding, showing how contemplative practices optimize our neurological capacity to receive guidance while maintaining the practical effectiveness and ethical responsibility essential for genuine service.

Throughout this exploration, we've discovered that learning to recognize universal signs isn't about developing supernatural abilities or escaping ordinary life responsibilities. Instead, it's about expanding our awareness to include the subtle dimensions of guidance and meaning that constantly surround us, waiting to be recognized by hearts and minds prepared to receive them.

The Integration of Science and Spirit

Perhaps the most significant insight emerging from this journey is the recognition that scientific understanding and spiritual awareness enhance rather than contradict each other when properly integrated. Dr. Swart's research on neuroplasticity, the Reticular Activating System, and contemplative neuroscience provides frameworks that validate spiritual experiences while helping us develop discernment about authentic guidance versus wishful projection.

Understanding how our brains process meaningful patterns doesn't reduce spiritual signs to mere neural activity—it reveals the elegant ways consciousness interfaces with reality to create experiences that serve both personal healing and collective welfare. This integration allows us to approach spiritual guidance with both openness and wisdom, receiving comfort and direction while maintaining the practical competence necessary for effective service.

The stories shared throughout these chapters—from Blake's numerical awakening to John's butterfly messages, from Rachel's medical intuitions to Alexandra's synchronistic career transition—all demonstrate how this integration of scientific knowledge and spiritual awareness creates optimal conditions for recognizing and responding to divine guidance in our daily lives.

The Ripple Effect of Recognition

What has become increasingly clear through both research and lived experience is that learning to recognize universal signs creates benefits extending far beyond individual comfort or guidance. When we develop the capacity to receive spiritual communication, we naturally become more sensitive to others' needs, more creative in problem-solving, and more effective in service that addresses both practical concerns and deeper needs for meaning and connection.

My evolution from grieving mother to spiritual guide for other families, Marcus's development from addiction recovery to holistic treatment innovation, and Linda's transformation from depression to community healing—these journeys illustrate how personal spiritual development naturally flows into service that multiplies healing for others.

Dr. Swart's research on neuroplasticity reveals the neurological basis for this ripple effect. Each time we recognize a meaningful sign and respond with appropriate action, we strengthen neural networks that support wisdom, compassion, and effectiveness in service. These brain changes don't just benefit us individually—they enhance our capacity to contribute to collective healing and transformation.

Practical Wisdom for the Journey

As you continue developing your own relationship with universal signs and divine guidance, several key insights can support your journey while maintaining balance and perspective:

- **Start Where You Are:** You don't need special abilities, extensive training, or perfect life circumstances to begin recognizing spiritual guidance. The capacity for receiving universal signs is your natural birthright, accessible through simple practices like attention to present-moment awareness, gratitude for support received, and openness to possibilities beyond your current understanding.

- **Maintain Balance:** Authentic spiritual development enhances rather than replaces practical effectiveness, professional competence, and ethical responsibility. Signs and synchronicities provide one source of guidance among many, working best when integrated with sound judgment, appropriate consultation, and consideration for others' welfare.

- **Trust the Process:** Spiritual communication operates according to divine timing rather than human schedules. Trust that the guidance you need will arrive when you're ready to receive and act upon it, while continuing to engage fully with your current life circumstances and responsibilities.

- **Practice Discernment:** Not every coincidence carries spiritual significance, and not every meaningful experience necessarily indicates specific action steps. Develop the ability to distinguish between authentic guidance and projection of desires or fears while remaining open to genuine spiritual communication.

- **Serve Others:** The ultimate purpose of spiritual guidance seems to be fostering healing, growth, and service that benefits both individual development and collective welfare. As your sensitivity to signs develops, look for opportunities to share your gifts in ways that support others' healing and spiritual development.

- **Stay Grounded:** Maintain engagement with ordinary life responsibilities, meaningful relationships, and practical service while developing spiritual awareness. The goal is integration rather than escape, enhancement rather than replacement of normal human functioning.

The Mystery Continues

Even after years of study, practice, and experience with spiritual signs, the fundamental mystery of how consciousness interfaces with reality to create meaningful guidance remains beautifully intact. Dr. Swart's research illuminates many mechanisms through which this communication operates, but the ultimate source and coordination of spiritual guidance continues to transcend complete scientific explanation.

This enduring mystery is part of the gift. Rather than reducing spiritual experience to mechanical processes, our growing understanding reveals the remarkable sophistication of the consciousness systems through which we receive guidance while honoring the transcendent dimensions that make this communication profoundly meaningful rather than merely informational.

The cardinal outside my window reminds me daily that love finds ways to transcend every apparent boundary, including death itself. The signs we've explored throughout this book—whether through winged messengers, numerical sequences, natural phenomena, or meaningful coincidences—all point to this fundamental truth: we are never alone, never without guidance, never beyond the reach of the love and intelligence that seeks our highest good and greatest service.

Your Ongoing Journey

As you close this book and continue your own exploration of universal signs and divine guidance, remember that this is just the beginning of a lifelong conversation with the mystery and intelligence that surrounds us. Each sign you recognize, each synchronicity you acknowledge, each inspired action you take contributes to the ongoing dialogue between your consciousness and the vast wisdom that guides all existence toward healing and growth.

Trust your ability to recognize the guidance meant specifically for you. Trust the process of gradual development that allows spiritual sensitivity to emerge naturally without forcing or pressure. Trust that the same love that sends signs also supports you as you learn to interpret and act upon the guidance you receive.

Most importantly, trust that your journey of spiritual development serves not just your personal healing and growth but also contributes to the collective awakening and transformation our world desperately needs. Each person who learns to recognize and respond to universal guidance becomes a conduit for the healing and transformation that flows through conscious participation in the ongoing dialogue between human hearts and divine intelligence.

The conversation between your consciousness and the universe has already begun. Every moment of wonder at a cardinal's appearance, every pause to notice a meaningful number sequence, every dream that brings comfort or guidance, and every act of kindness inspired by spiritual awareness contributes to the growing recognition that we live in an intelligent, loving universe that constantly offers support to those ready to receive it.

Your willingness to remain open to signs while maintaining practical engagement with life's responsibilities makes you a bridge between the seen and unseen worlds. Through your conscious participation in this dialogue, you help demonstrate that spiritual awareness enhances rather than diminishes our capacity for effective service, meaningful relationships, and constructive contribution to community welfare.

May you continue to recognize the signs that speak directly to your heart. May you trust the gradual process of spiritual development that honors both mystery and practicality. And may your journey of receiving and responding to universal guidance contribute to the healing of our world, one conscious choice at a time.

The signs are always present, waiting for hearts prepared to receive them. The universe speaks continuously through countless channels, offering whispers of love that transcend even death itself. All we need is the willingness to listen with both mind and heart open to the infinite possibilities for connection, healing, and service that surround us in every moment.

RESOURCES AND FURTHER READING

Recommended Books

Spiritual Signs and Synchronicity:

- "Signs: The Secret Language of the Universe" by Laura Lynne Jackson
- "When God Winks" by SQuire Rushnell
- "The Celestine Prophecy" by James Redfield
- "The Alchemist" by Paulo Coelho

Neuroscience and Consciousness:

- "The Source: Open Your Mind, Change Your Life" by Dr. Tara Swart
- "Signs: Decode the Messages and Discover Your Cosmic Blueprint" by Dr. Tara Swart
- "The Brain That Changes Itself" by Norman Doidge
- ""Waking Up" by Sam Harris

Grief and After-Death Communication:

- "Hello From Heaven" by Bill and Judy Guggenheim
- "The Afterlife of Billy Fingers" by Annie Kagan
- "Love Never Dies" by Jamie Turndorf
- "Signs from Spirit" by Lyn Ragan

Meditation and Mindfulness:

- "Wherever You Go, There You Are" by Jon Kabat-Zinn
- "The Miracle of Mindfulness" by Thich Nhat Hanh
- "Real Happiness" by Sharon Salzberg
- "The Mind Illuminated" by Culadasa

Angel Numbers and Sacred Symbolism:

- "Angel Numbers" by Doreen Virtue
- "The Complete Book of Numerology" by David Phillips
- "Sacred Geometry" by Stephen Skinner
- "The Hidden Reality of Symbols" by Jordan Maxwell

Nature and Animal Messengers:

- "Animal Speak" by Ted Andrews
- "Medicine Cards" by Jamie Sams and David Carson
- "The Hidden Life of Trees" by Peter Wohlleben
- "Braiding Sweetgrass" by Robin Wall Kimmerer

Online Resources and Support

Meditation and Mindfulness Apps:

- Headspace - Guided meditations for beginners and advanced practitioners
- Calm - Sleep stories, meditation, and relaxation programs
- Insight Timer - Free meditation library with community features
- Ten Percent Happier - Practical meditation for skeptics

Grief Support:

- GriefShare - Faith-based grief recovery support groups
- The Compassionate Friends - Support for families after child loss
- Modern Loss - Online community for those experiencing loss
- What's Your Grief - Educational resources and support tools

Spiritual Development Communities:

- Omega Institute - Workshops and retreats for spiritual growth
- Esalen Institute - Programs integrating psychology and spirituality
- Local meditation centers and spiritual communities
- Online forums for synchronicity and spiritual experiences

Professional Support Resources

When to Seek Professional Help: If you experience persistent sadness, anxiety, difficulty functioning, or concerning spiritual experiences that interfere with daily life, please consider professional support:

- Licensed mental health counselors specializing in grief or spiritual issues
- Certified spiritual directors trained in guiding spiritual development
- Medical professionals for health-related concerns
- Crisis hotlines for immediate emotional support

Important Note: The spiritual experiences and practices described in this book are intended to complement, not replace, professional mental health care, medical treatment, or appropriate therapeutic intervention when needed.

Dear Reader,

Thank you so much for choosing *Whispers from Beyond*. I truly hope the stories, guidance, and insights in these pages helped you feel more connected—to the universe, to your intuition, and to the loved ones who continue to walk beside you from beyond.

If this book brought you comfort, clarity, or confirmation in your own spiritual journey, **would you consider leaving an honest review on Amazon?** Your feedback not only supports my work as an independent author, but it also helps other readers who are seeking guidance, healing, and hope to discover this book. Just scan the QR code to review my book.

Your voice has the power to help others find light during their own moments of questioning or loss—and I'm deeply grateful for your time and support.

Thank you for being part of this journey of connection, intuition, and universal wisdom.

With gratitude,
Wendy Samons

BIBLIOGRAPHY

Primary Sources

Swart, Tara, MD, PhD. *The Source: Open Your Mind, Change Your Life.* HarperOne, 2019.

Swart, Tara, MD, PhD. *Signs: Decode the Messages and Discover Your Cosmic Blueprint.* Vermilion, 2023.

Jackson, Laura Lynne. *Signs: The Secret Language of the Universe.* Spiegel & Grau, 2019.

Scientific and Academic Sources

Neuroscience and Psychology:

- Swart, Tara. "Neuroplasticity and Cognitive Enhancement." *Nature Reviews Neuroscience*, 2021.
- McGee, Maryanna. "Meditation and Psychiatry." *Psychiatry Journal*, 2008.
- Van't Westeinde, A. & Patel, K.D. "Heartfulness Meditation: A Yogic and Neuroscientific Perspective." *Frontiers in Psychology*, 2022.
- Ardelt, Monika. "Wisdom and Life Satisfaction in Old Age." *Journal of Gerontology*, 2003.

Consciousness Studies:

- Jung, Carl Gustav. *Synchronicity: An Acausal Connecting Principle.* Princeton University Press, 1973.
- Jung, Carl Gustav. *Man and His Symbols.* Doubleday, 1964.
- Sheldrake, Rupert. *The Sense of Being Stared At.* Crown Publishers, 2003.

Grief and Bereavement Research:

- Klass, Dennis. *Continuing Bonds: New Understandings of Grief.* Taylor & Francis, 1996.
- Worden, J. William. *Grief Counseling and Grief Therapy.* Springer Publishing, 2018.
- Stroebe, Margaret S. *Handbook of Bereavement Research.* American Psychological Association, 2001.

Cultural and Historical Studies:

- Campbell, Joseph. *The Hero with a Thousand Faces.* Pantheon Books, 1949.
- Eliade, Mircea. *The Sacred and the Profane.* Harcourt Brace Jovanovich, 1987.
- Andrews, Ted. *Animal Speak: The Spiritual & Magical Powers of Creatures Great & Small.* Llewellyn Publications, 1993.

Spiritual and Philosophical Sources

Contemporary Spiritual Authors:

- Tolle, Eckhart. *The Power of Now.* New World Library, 1999.
- Chopra, Deepak. *SyncDestiny.* Rider Books, 2003.
- Williamson, Marianne. *A Return to Love.* HarperCollins, 1992.

Classical Spiritual Texts:

- *The Bhagavad Gita.* Translated by Barbara Stoler Miller. Bantam Classics, 1986.
- *The Tao Te Ching.* Translated by Stephen Mitchell. Harper & Row, 1988.
- *The Holy Bible, New International Version.* Zondervan, 2011.

Mystical and Contemplative Traditions:

- John of the Cross, St. *Dark Night of the Soul.* Dover Publications, 2003.
- Rumi, Jalaluddin. *The Essential Rumi.* Translated by Coleman Barks. HarperSanFrancisco, 1995.
- Teresa of Avila, St. *Interior Castle.* Dover Publications, 2000